SELECT GREEK COINS

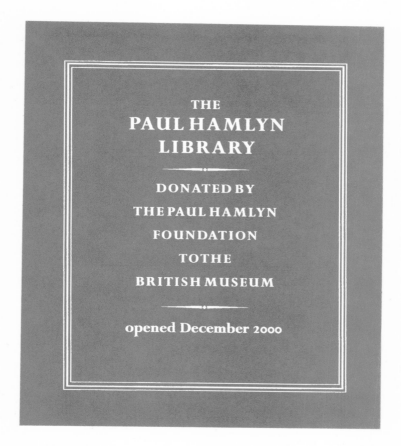

SELECT
GREEK COINS

A SERIES OF ENLARGEMENTS
ILLUSTRATED AND DESCRIBED

BY

GEORGE F. HILL

KEEPER OF COINS AND MEDALS, BRITISH MUSEUM

———

PARIS AND BRUSSELS

LIBRAIRIE NATIONALE D'ART ET D'HISTOIRE

G. VANOEST, PUBLISHER

—

1927

PREFACE

This book is an experiment. Magnified reproductions of single ancient coins have not infrequently been published, but no attempt has been made hitherto to present a long series of such magnifications. There are objections to this, as there are to most experiments. To enlarge the work of a die-engraver three diameters is to put his skill to a cruel test. He never intended that his coins should be looked at under such conditions. Yet every day and nearly all day long numismatists are using their magnifying-glasses on his products. So that he has no choice. And if he runs the risk of his work failing under the test, he has a splendid reward when it passes muster, and the large sculptural qualities of his tiny relief come out on a scale on which they can be appreciated by everyone without microscopic eyes.

Here will be found all sorts of coins from the sixth to the first century B. C. Some have borne enlargement better than might have been expected; in others, like the Rhodian tetradrachm (pl. V, no 5), what seemed to be boldness of style has revealed itself as something like a staring shamelessness; or in others, like the Antiochus VI (pl. XVII, no. 1) the shallowness of the workmanship is betrayed by the way in which the whole design has gone to pieces; or, as in the Augustan sphinx (pl. LX, no. 4), the meagreness of the technique comes out in unhappy contrast with the fine solidity of its Chian predecessor (pl. LX, no. 1). But, taking it as whole, the book will, I trust, increase the reputation of the Greek die-engraver, and be useful as giving a fairly long series of dated works of art. At least I take courage from the remark of an archaeologist who, on seeing the plates for the first time, exclaimed that he had never really *seen* Greek coins before, though he had often looked at them.

The designs are arranged roughly according to subject, and chronologically under each subject : male heads, female heads, single figures, figures grouped with animals, chariot-groups, animals, monstrous beings, plants, and inanimate objects. But the arrangement has not been followed logically ; thus for instance, satyrs and winged figures have escaped from the class of monstrous into that of normal beings. Anyone to whom it may seem worth while can find other examples of such inconsistency.

In the case of four coins, no longer within reach, the photographs have been made from electrotypes. The present owners of two (pl. XXVIII, no. 1, LVIII, no. 2, LXI, no. 1) being unknown to me, I have ventured to assume their permission. All the others have been photographed direct from the originals.

My thanks are due to my colleague Mr. Stanley Robinson for much good counsel, and to those collectors who have kindly allowed me to illustrate specimens in their collections, viz. Captain E. G. Spencer-Churchill, Mr. C. S. Gulbenkian, M. Robert Jameson, Mr. A. H. Lloyd, Mr. Stanley Robinson, Mr. J. I. S. Whitaker and Mr. W. H. Woodward. All the other coins illustrated are in the British Museum.

G. F. H.
British Museum
October 1925.

SELECT GREEK COINS

INTRODUCTION

The development of coins as works of art is a subject that cannot be considered in detail in a short space and without a full illustrative apparatus. [1] A few general remarks are all that can be made here. There is of course no reason why the coin should be a work of art ; its purpose as a medium of exchange can be equally well served by a plain disk of metal bearing on its surface the necessary information ; and such a coinage would be less discreditable than the futile attempts at an artistic currency which are all that most modern nations seem able to produce. Mechanical methods of reproduction are now so efficient, that one great reason for an elaborately modelled design — the difficulty of imitation by the forger — is no longer of force.

But the Greeks of the great period were naturally incapable of neglecting the artistic possibilities of any object in daily use, and to that fact we owe it that among their coins are to be found innumerable masterpieces of art. The history of Greek coinage, it is true, contradicts some of our most cherished maxims concerning the decoration of objects of common use. We are told, for instance, that such an object is beautiful if it is made in the form most efficient for its purpose. But the one thing that is clear to the honest observer of the history of Greek coinage is that, throughout the period when Greek art was at its finest, the decoration of the coins was in no way helpful from the practical point of view ; or, perhaps it would be fairer to say, the method of decoration

---

1. On the subject, so far as concerns Greek coins, consult especially P. Gardner, *Types of Greek Coins* (Cambridge, 1882) ; B. V. Head, *Guide to the principal Gold and Silver Coins of the Ancients* (2d. ed., London, 1881) ; and K. Regling, *Die Münze als Kunstwerk* (Berlin, 1924).

was such that inevitably, the more the coin was used for its proper purpose, the more it suffered. The story is that of a continual struggle to reconcile with practical requirements an incompatible artistic ideal. It was left for the Middle Ages to solve the problem which had baffled the Greek ; and, unfortunately, the lesson of the Middle Ages is entirely lost upon the modern die-engraver.

The idea of a coin-type arose out of a signet, which was impressed in soft material from a deeply engraved seal. Since the impression of a seal was not required to circulate from hand to hand or to be subjected to wear in any other way, the height of its relief did not matter. But as the coin circulated, the relief was bound to suffer ; the very idea of any but the most moderate relief is accordingly alien to the idea of a coin. Signets were in use from time immemorial, and preceded the use of writing or the engraving of inscriptions. It is very probable that had epigraphy been in general use at the time of the invention of coinage, and had the inventors not been a people who thought and felt more in plastic than in graphic or in literary form, had they not, in fact, been born sculptors, the history of coinage would have been very different. We might have had something like the decorative patterns in low relief of the end of the Middle Ages, or like the fine calligraphic designs of those peoples whose religion forbids them the representation of living creatures.

We may be thankful, however, that the Greeks allowed their artistic instincts to overrule any such practical considerations. They seized the opportunity of making each coin a small work of art in relief. At first there were technical difficulties to be triumphed over. Beyond the initial one, common to the arts of the die-engraver and the gem-engraver, of cutting the design in reverse in a hard material, there was the problem of impressing it on a material only less refractory. In order to do this, the upper die had to be driven with force into the upper side of the blank, so as to make the metal fill the lower die. This produced an incuse impression, usually square or circular. It was only upon second thoughts that a second design was engraved on the upper or reverse die. The reverse design was at first framed within the incuse impression. This had what moderns might regard as the advantage that one side, at least, of the coin was comparatively well protected from wear. But the Greeks, characteristically, cared nothing for such protection, and their efforts were continuously directed towards doing away with the incuse square or circle. The first reverse designs, properly speaking, such as the owl at Athens, appeared in the first half of the sixth century ; but it was not until the beginning of the fourth that the marked incuse impression gave way to a slight concavity of the reverse surface, which was preserved during the whole of the time that Greek coins made any pretence to artistic quality. A deliberate revival of the marked incuse square, which took place in one or two coinages, in Rhodes, Caria and Lycia, in the second century B. C., was due merely to some archaistic fancy.

The majority of the early coins are comparatively thick. There are, it is true, certain series of Euboea and Macedonia, as well as the earliest coins of Corinth and of the Achaean Colonies in South Italy, which favour a flat fabric. But the thick 'dump' is by far the commonest type of coin until the end of the third century B. C. After that there begins, especially in Asia Minor and Syria, a tendency to strike what are known as the spread tetradrachms, with a well-placed design in a fairly broad field. This is the most showy, though not the highest, development of the Greek die-engraver's art ; it compares in quality with the art of the fifth century, as in England the gorgeous Tudor gold coinage with the far finer productions of the time of Edward III.

Modelling in one form or another being of the essence of the art of ancient coins, we may note one or two points regarding its development and the methods adopted for treating details. They can only be properly appreciated by handling the originals or mechanical facsimiles ; photographs are apt to mislead owing to the forcing of shadows or other distortions.

The influence of gem-engraving is particularly evident in the modelling of many early coins, even though the instrument used for engraving was not a drill, but a punch or scauper. If we examine, for instance, the helmeted head on the early coins of Calymnos, of the sixth century, [1] we see that certain features, such as the point of the nasal of the helmet, the point of the nose itself, the eye, the left nostril, are rendered by round blobs which stand out prominently from their surroundings, the gradation into which is practically unattempted. Similar treatment is visible on a coin of Lete ; [2] in the figure of the satyr who is seizing a nymph, his cheek, right shoulder, biceps, right buttock and knee-joints have all been made in the same way, and not worked up so as to grade into the surrounding portions of the surface. Generally speaking, it is characteristic of all the earliest die-engraver's art that he conscientiously records the various details of the anatomy, but fails to coordinate them, and give them the continuous surface which they have in nature. He is at the opposite pole to the artists of the

1. Head, *Guide*, pl. 3, no. 29.
2. *Ibid.*, pl. 4, no. 5.

G. F. HILL. — *Select Greek Coins.*   2

decline, who have ceased to care about the anatomical structure of a body, and produce a smooth and polished surface which appears to have no substance beneath it. [1]

As time goes on, he becomes more skilful, but the gradations continue to give him trouble, and it is long before he masters the problem of treating the lips so that they do not look like two sharp ridges rising from the face. On the Demareteion of 480 B. C. (pl. XX, no. 1) he has succeeded in making the lips full — the larger scale of the coin has given him a chance — but the gradation from the front of the face to the cheek is still imperfect. That pride in anatomical knowledge, which shows itself even at a comparatively late period in some schools of sculpture, as in the Amazon frieze of the Maussolleum, is partly responsible for such exaggeration of the drawing of the muscles as we find in the earlier tetradrachms of Sicilian Naxos (pl. XXXVIII, no. 1). The coins of this place are particularly interesting, showing as they do how the artist of the later tetradrachm (Pl. XL, no. 2) softened in all respects the modelling of his predecessor of a generation earlier. On the earlier coin the treatment of the Silenus's belly is almost like an attempt at an anatomical figure, with the skin removed. It can be paralleled on many an early fifth century gem, but more especially on the Etruscan, [2] where, however, the anatomy, though paraded, is not understood.

The treatment of the eye is naturally one of the chief difficulties of the primitive artist. In the profile head he represents it as if it were seen full ; and he has mastered none of the subtle modelling which is necessary to prevent a staring effect. On the coin of Calymnos already mentioned the iris is strongly emphasized. On many of the sixth century 'owls' of Athens, [3] however, it is barely indicated ; the eye looks like a nearly flat patch laid on the face and surrounded by, but not lower than, a moulding representing the lids. On the earliest, sixth century, coins of Sicilian Naxos, [4] the eye is treated as a kind of elongated swelling within the eye-socket ; it is probably an accident that gives it the appearance of looking downwards, with a sneering expression. The Sicilian artists were, however, much in advance of the Greeks of Greece Proper ; even before 480 the eye on some Syracusan coins (pl. XIX, no.2), with all

1. Examples are the popular coins of Philistis of Syracuse (pl. XXXVI, no. 3) or the large tetradrachms of places like Smyrna and Cyme (Pl. XXXVI, no. 1). Even Euaenetus, the famous Syracusan engraver of an earlier age, does not escape a certain emptiness in this respect (pl. XXVIII, no. 1).

2. See J. D. Beazley, *Lewes House Collection of Gems*, pl. 9, nos 27, 31 (Greek), 39, 40, 41, 43 (Etruscan) and 13 (Greco-Phoenician).

3. Head, *op. cit.*, pl. 6, nos. 27 and 28. But these are not among the earliest, many of which indicate the iris, e. g. Seltman, *Athens*, pl. II and III.

4. Head, *op. cit.*, pl. 9, no. 31.

its faults, has a quite natural expression ; there is an attempt to model the iris. On the Demareteion (pl. XX, no. 1) the iris is defined, and there is some modelling of the upper lid ; even the lower eyelashes are slightly indicated. Immediately after this time the engravers realised that the eye in a profile head should be seen in profile. [1] Many of them also, unfortunately, attempted to represent the eyelashes in greater profusion ; but the absurdity of the effect except in the most skilful hands was soon patent, and the practice was abandoned, or confined to the indication of a single hair. [2]

Another feature, the development in the treatment of which is worth following through its primitive stages, is the hair of the head, Here two instruments, the round-headed punch and the graver, are used to represent curliness or straightness respectively. On the earlier 'owls' of Athens, [3] for instance, the fringe of hair on the forehead is usually treated in slightly curved lines, each ending in a little pellet, representing a round curl ; sometimes, however, the whole of the front hair is shown as a mass of little pellets ; and on these coins even the long lines of the hair hanging under the neck-piece of Athena's helmet are done not with the graver but with the punch, in rows of pellets (cp. pl. XIX, no. 1). The head of Dionysus on the earliest coin of Naxos already mentioned has the beard done with the graver, the hair on the forehead with the punch. But on the Syracusan tetradrachm of the earliest years of the fifth century [4] the artist has adopted an inverse arrangement — graver for the forehead hair, punch for all the rest. The same use of the dotting-punch, on a much finer scale, however, and manipulated with great delicacy, characterizes the early fifth-century heads on the coins of Corinth (pl. XIX, no. 4) and Cnidus (pl. XX, no. 4). At Athens the rendering of the hair of the forehead by wavy lines ending in little curls goes on until after the time of Marathon, but on the coins issued after that victory it begins to be superseded by a more naturalistic waving of the hair. The dotting-punch, however, continues to be used, even down to the fourth century, for the hair which appears under the neck-piece. It must be remembered that the Athenian coinage, after the really archaic period, was deliberately archaistic.

Of more importance to the modern designer than the treatment of details by the primitive craftsmen is the lesson which ancient coins provide in the matter of the posing

1. The coins on pl. XX ff. illustrate the results of this discovery. The heads on the two tetradrachms of Naxos already mentioned (pl. I, no. 2, II, no. 1) also show the transition from half to true profile.
2. On the representation of the eyelashes on fifth-century gems and coins see J. D. Beazley, *op. cit.*, p. 47.
3. British Museum Catalogue, *Attica*, pl. I.
4. Head, *Guide*, pl. 9, no. 35.

of the head as a whole. Generally speaking, the Greek artist avoided the facing posi-tion. It is, as a matter of fact, quite unsuitable to coinage, except in the very lowest relief ; [1] but the Greeks, with their delightful carelessness about practical matters, were slow in discovering this. It is obvious that, since the nose of a facing head is the first detail to suffer in circulation, such a design rapidly becomes a caricature ; whereas a profile, which depends so much on contour for its effect, may suffer much abrasion of the higher planes before its character is destroyed. There are a few early coins which adopt an absolutely frontal treatment in high relief, but for the most part the artists of this period were content with the profile. When, however, towards the end of the fifth century, the Greek engravers had attained a high degree of skill, they were tempted and fell. In many mints, in Magna Graecia, in Greece Proper, and in Asia Minor, facing heads, with very slight inclination from absolute frontality, were attempted. At Syra-cuse, the engraver Kimon produced his extremely popular Arethusa (pl. XXVII, no. 5). As it was greatly admired by the Greeks (witness the copies of it produced at Larisa in Thessaly and at Tarsus in Cilicia), there is every excuse for those moderns who regard it as the most beautiful of ancient coins. Its sensuous attraction is undeniable ; but it lacks dignity and restraint and intellectual quality, and we cannot imagine the artists of Olympia attempting such a rendering of their Hera, or even of their nymph Olympia. The facing head of Athena by Eucleidas of Syracuse (pl. XXVII, no. 1) is on a higher plane, though still too florid to be monumental ; and the same exuberance charac-terizes and spoils the heads of Apollo by Heracleidas (pl. V, no. 1) and Choirion at Catana. The latter artist adopts absolute frontality, resulting in an unpleasant star-ing effect. These are the more important Sicilian efforts in this direction ; all date from the end of the fifth century. The fashion was copied in certain mints of South Italy dur-ing the fourth century ; the heads of nymphs at Naples and Phistelia may indeed have preceded Kimon's work.

In Southern Greece Proper, the fashion was almost unknown after the early coins mentioned above. But it was in Northern Greece and in Asia Minor that the most interesting attempts at the treatment were made. The bold but unintellectual head of Hermes at Aenus (pl. V, no. 2), the beautiful but rather effeminate head of Apollo at Amphipolis (pl. VI, no. 1), the highly emotional head of the same god at Clazomenae (pl. V, no. 4), and the sensuous conception of Helios at Rhodes (pl. V, nos 3, 5), all

---

1. Except also for such caricatures as the Gorgon mask, for which it was the standard treatment (pl. LIX, nos. 4, 5) ; or as the facing head of Silenus on small coins of Catana (Hill, *Ancient Sicily*, pl. IX, 6).

dating from the finest period, i. e. from the end of the fifth or the beginning of the fourth century B. C., have much more character than the efforts of the Western Greeks. So too have the heads of a satyr at Panticapaeum (pl. VIII, no. 4) and of Ammon at Cyrene (pl. VI, no. 2).

Although artists in most parts of the ancient world continued from time to time, down to the first century B. C., to make experiments in the facing head, their achievements, after the fine period, are of small artistic interest.

The frontal pose for objects more complex than a single head or a single figure is a rarity ; and even though single figures are often found standing to front, the head is generally turned to one side. A very curious attempt at solving a problem of this kind was made at Corinth in the second half of the fifth century. Here, on a quite small coin, [1] we have a design, five-sixteenths of an inch or eight millimetres in height, of Pegasus prancing on his hind legs, seen from the front. The head is in profile, and so, apparently, are the two hind legs, but the wings are displayed, and there is a distinct attempt at foreshortening the body. It is curious that so original a treatment should be found on a minor denomination like the diobol. There are, indeed, very few instances of real foreshortening to be found on ancient Greek coins ; squatting figures like the satyr of Sicilian Naxos already mentioned (pl. XXXVIII, no. 1, XL, no. 2), or the infant Heracles strangling the snakes on coins of a number of mints early in the fourth century, are arranged with certain conventions so as to avoid the necessity of foreshortening the limbs. Even the skill of Sicilian engravers did not embolden them to tackle the problem ; how they shirked it may be seen on the famous decadrachm of Agrigentum (pl. LI, no. 2), where the only indication of the fact that the chariot is making a sharp turn is that the wheels are rendered in perspective, whereas the horses are in profile. A true example is, however, found in the bull on certain coins of Gortyna (pl. LV, no. 4), where the influence of painting may account for the artist's audacity. The only parallel to such treatment on Greek coins — and it is but a partial parallel — is found in the three-quarters view of the head and neck of a bull on other coins of Gortyna [2] and more or less contemporary coins of Euboea. [3]

The study of the composition of the coin-types of the Greeks shows that they attempt-

1. British Museum Catalogue, *Corinth*, pl. II, no. 25.
2. British Museum Catalogue, *Crete*, pl. IX, no. 10, XI, no. 3.
3. British Museum Catalogue, *Central Greece*, pl. XVII, no. 6. One should perhaps add an early Etruscan coin with the head and neck of a bull.

ed, if not always with success, to solve most of the problems involved in the arrangement of circular designs. The artist who has to deal with a single head has a comparatively simple task, although there are few who attain the miraculous success in the mere posing of the bust within a circular field which is seen in the medals of Pisanello. But when he has to represent a complete figure, human or animal, or a group of figures, the primitive artist, who does not like vacant spaces, resorts to all kinds of devices to fit his design to the round. He may call in aid adjuncts, separate from the main type, or, when he becomes literate, inscriptions to fill the field. But if he has not these accessories, we find him posing his figures in conventional attitudes to suit his purpose. A bull is shown with its head turned back towards its flank (pl. LIV, no. 4) ; or a human figure is placed in the 'kneeling-running' pose (pl. XXXVII, no. 3). The artlessness of the archaic designers in the use of such conventions is manifest. The artists of a riper age are of course more skilful. On the staters of Cyzicus, for instance, we may notice how frequently the figures are put into attitudes which, though perfectly unconstrained, are obviously more suitable than an upright position for the circular shape of the coin. Of nineteen figure-subjects chosen at random [1], eight are kneeling or crouching ; one, Triptolemus, is in a chariot drawn by winged snakes ; Gaia holding Erichthonius is seen in half figure rising from the earth ; Cecrops has the lower, serpentine half of his body coiled up ; a satyr sits on the ground, Thetis on her dolphin ; Heracles kneels to wrestle with the lion ; Taras rides on his dolphin ; an infant squats on the ground ; an armed runner stoops and stretches out his hand, about to begin the race ; and Harmodius and Aristogeiton rush forward together, left arms outstretched, right hands drawn back holding daggers. As Gardner has remarked, [2] we find on the Cyzicene staters a kneeling Helios, and even " a kneeling Zeus, a type which one must almost see to believe in it. " In all the Cyzicene series there are only two full-length standing figures [3] ; yet not one of the types is anything but naturally posed.

But this was at the finest period of the Greek coinage. To return to the primitive designer, he very early becomes skilled in the use of adjuncts and inscriptions ; thus the design of Apollo on the early coins of Caulonia (pl. XXXVII, no. 1), with the little winged figure on his outstretched left arm, the stag standing in front of him, and the four letters of the inscription behind, all surrounded by a cable border, is a fine specimen

1. British Museum Catalogue, *Mysia*, pl. VI and VII.
2. *Types of Greek Coins*, p. 67.
3. *Nomisma*, VII (1912), pl. VI, nos. 12, 15 ; Babelon, *Traité des Monnaies grecques et romaines*, pl. CLXXIV, no. 42 ; pl. CLXXV, no. 2.

of satisfactory primitive design. Sometimes the adjuncts seem to be purely ornamental space-fillers : such are the palmette and strip of guilloche pattern which accompany the eagle's head on coins of Paphos, [1] modelled on earlier coins of Ialysus, which have an inscription instead of the guilloche. The modification of the circle by cutting off an 'exergue' by a straight line, on which a figure or group might be made to stand, was an obvious device, which has lasted down to the present day. The use of inscriptions as an element of the design was quickly seized upon. A fine example of simple but effective use is seen at Poseidonia, where two straight lines of letters stand on either side of the striding figure of Poseidon (pl. XXXVIII, no. 3). Except in the West, where, especially in Sicily, a circular inscription was very commonly used from the earliest times, and in Egypt, where the Ptolemies also affected the circular arrangement, the Greeks seem to have preferred as a rule to dispose the lettering in straight lines. The circular inscription, which seems so natural to us, is not really common until Roman times. When the Greeks used a long inscription as a border, they liked to place it along the sides of a square. Thus it might be placed, as we have seen it on the early coins of Poseidonia, on the left and right of a standing or seated figure, or on one side and below, or on left and right and below, or, finally, on all four sides. This arrangement is carried to excess on the coins of the Parthian kings, who, to find room for the string of grandiose titles which they affected, sometimes enclosed the design of the reverse in a double square of inscription, containing no less than eight titles.

So far we have considered mainly types consisting of single heads or figures. But there is also the problem of composing a design containing two or more heads or figures. For the most part the coin-designs seem to tell us nothing more than any other works of art about the way in which the Greeks grappled with such subjects. Groups, in some respects, offer less difficulty than single figures when the field is circular, so far as the problem is merely one of getting the design to fill the field of itself. Medieval art tended to heraldic opposition. Roman art, when it was not intent on a narrative treatment, staked all on mechanical symmetry, the Emperor (like his artistic heirs, Christ and the Virgin) taking a central position, with supporters balancing each other on either side. Greek art had known from the beginning [2] the principle of heraldic opposition, and rejected it for the very good reason that it gave limited play to the intellect, which

---

1. British Museum Catalogue, *Cyprus*, pl. VII, nos. 4-9.
2. Ernst Curtius, *Ueber Wappengebrauch und Wappenstil im griech. Altertum* (*Gesammelte Abhandl.*, ii, 1894, pp. 77-115).

the Greeks regarded as the controlling factor in art. [1] It was the Romans who developed the principle of static symmetry, in the sense which demands a central figure to which supporters do service. [2] Greek composition, on the contrary, was based on a dynamic principle, which produced movement and rhythm instead of mechanical balance. It is interesting to find this principle asserting itself in some of the rare cases in which, in developed Greek art, an approach is made to heraldic arrangement. On the coins of Istrus, [3] for instance, the engravers have to represent two heads. Instead of placing them facing merely side by side, or confronted, or addorsed, they invert one as regards the other. Similarly when the Thasian engraver represents two wine-jars, he places one of them upside down. [4] It is to be doubted whether there is any symbolical significance in this queer arrangement ; it is probably prompted merely by a distaste for mechanical symmetry. Perhaps the best example of all, however, is the strange coin of some unidentified city of Asia Minor, on which we have the foreparts of a winged horse and a winged lion conjoined at the shoulders, looking different ways, but one of them inverted as regards the other, so that they give an impression of whirling round. The effect is all the more striking when compared with another Asiatic coin, also of uncertain origin, in which the foreparts of a lion and a bull looking different ways are conjoined in the ordinary — but not particularly Greek — manner. [5] Almost always the Greek, if he has to express opposition, prefers to express at the same time movement, not mere blockade. A fairly common type is composed of two dolphins. Instead of balancing them by making them swim in the same direction, belly to belly, he usually makes them swim in opposite directions, one under the other, as on the early coins of Thera ; [6] or chase each other in a circle, as on the fourth century coins of Argos. [7]

There are nevertheless a certain number of examples of more or less heraldic opposition to be found on Greek coins of various periods. On an electrum coin struck at some

1. E. Strong, *Apotheosis* ; G. F. Hill, *Christus Imperator*, in *Burlington Magazine*, Apr. 1916, pp. 21ff.

2. Good examples of mechanical symmetry on these lines are the coins of Ephesus on which the idol of the Ephesian Artemis stands between the two river-gods Cayster and Cenchrius, or behind an altar at which the Emperors Marcus Aurelius and Lucius Verus do sacrifice (British Museum Catalogue, *Ionia*, pl. XIII, nos. 8 and 12). These are the work of degenerate Greek artists working under the Roman dominion.

3. B. Pick, *Ant. Münzen von Dacien und Moesien*, i (1898), Taf. II, nos. 20f.

4. Regling, *Sammlung Warren*, Taf. XIII, no. 505.

5. Babelon, *Traité*, pl. XXVIII, no. 10 and II, no. 3. The two coins are placed side by side in Gardner's *Types*, pl. IV, nos. 13 and 14.

6. Babelon, *Traité*, pl. LXII, nos. 16-20.

7. Head, *Guide*, pl. 23, no. 36.

Ionian city in the late sixth or early fifth century we have two rampant lions opposed, with some object between them, at once recalling the Lion Gate at Mycenae. [1] On a coin of the beginning of the fifth century struck at some unidentified Macedonian town [2] two nymphs support an amphora. One of the best examples is the arrangement of two rams' heads and two dolphins on a rare tridrachm of Delphi, about 480 B. C. [3] In the latter half of the sixth century Lesbos issued base metal coins with a tree between two calves' heads opposed. [4] But this is not the place for a complete enumeration of such designs.

We have already noticed one somewhat fantastic treatment of a type consisting of two heads. All the more ordinary methods of dealing with such types were also tried by the ancient designers. One, which has taken its name from the double-faced god Janus, is seen as early as the middle of the sixth century on coins of Tenedos, [5] where on the obverse a janiform head, the one side male, the other female, corresponds to the reverse type of a double axe. To the early fifth century belong drachms of Lampsacus [6] on which both faces of the janiform head are beardless and presumably female. But the commonest of all examples is of course the bearded Janus himself, on the Roman as, which was first issued about 335 B. C. We need not trace its history further on Roman coins.

Two other methods of placing a pair of heads need hardly be mentioned here. The jugate or accollate position apparently does not occur before the third century B. C. One of the earliest instances is on the gold coins struck, with the heads of Ptolemy I and Berenice on one side, and those of Ptolemy II and Arsinoe on the other, in the reign of the latter pair (285-247 B. C.). [7] The heads of the Dioscuri on the coins of the Brettii belong to about the same time. Other examples from Greek coins of the second and first century could be cited ; but the great vogue of the pose belongs to the Roman Empire.

Similarly, the confronted pose, being easier to execute, and in harmony with the Roman idea of symmetry, is very popular on Roman Imperial coins. It is difficult, if not impossible, to cite an example from Greek coinage before Roman times.

Every artist knows that the border or frame of a composition is no unimportant

1. *Journal of Hellenic Studies*, xvii, 1897, pl. II, no. 3. Regling, *Die Münze als Kunstwerk*, pl. I, no. 7.
2. British Museum Catalogue, *Thrace*, p. 135. Babelon, *Traité*, pl. LVIII, no. 2. Regling, pl. IV, no. 96.
3. Head, *Historia Numorum*, 2d. ed., p. 340 ; Babelon, pl. XLII, no. 16. Regling, pl. VII, no. 189.
4. British Museum Catalogue, *Troas*, pl. XXX, no. 20.
5. Head, *Guide*, pl. I, no. 19.
6. Head, *Guide*, pl. 2, no 18.
7. Head, *Guide*, pl. 40, no. 1.

factor in the total effect. A few words will therefore be in place here concerning the various kinds of border employed by the ancients. Frequently, and on many of the best coins, they dispensed with anything of the kind, allowing the edge of the coin itself to serve as the boundary of their design. On the reverses, in the period before the disappearance of the incuse impression, that is, generally speaking, before the end of the fifth century, the rising edge of metal left outside the impression of the reverse die effectively limited the field (see, for instance, pl. XL, no. 3). A curious effect was occasionally produced by shaping the die so that this edge conformed to the general outline of the type. The best known example of this fancy is on the very early coins of Calymnos with the lyre. [1]

Of actual borders the most common is that known to English cataloguers as the border of dots, or pearled border. [2] It is frequently, especially on coins of the severe period, used to line the edge of the incuse impression (pl. XXXVII, no. 6). It is much commoner than the plain linear circle, although such a circle was very commonly drawn, with compasses or otherwise, as a guide to the placing of the dots, which were made in the die with an ordinary round-headed punch. When the dots are not placed so close together as to obliterate the linear circle, the appearance is that of a string of beads (pl. XXVII, no. 5). The punch used for making the border was however not always round-headed, but shaped like a long oval or the section of a double convex lens. The result was a border composed of a series of what look like flat beads placed side to side. This is especially common on Byzantine coins. [3]

When these beads, reduced to mere dashes, are placed slanting, we get a spiral wire effect ; instances are rare in Greek coins, though it is found in the fifth century, [4] but it is not uncommon on Byzantine coins. [5]

A triple pearled circle occurs on a fifth century coin of Poseidonia, [6] but so poverty-stricken a device is rare on Greek coins ; a double or triple beaded circle is very common on eighth century Byzantine coins from Constantine V (741-775) onwards [7].

The plain linear circle is, as stated, less common on Greek coins than the pearled,

1. Head, *Guide*, pl. 3, no. 29.
2. French *grènetis*, [tal. *granitura*, Germ. *Perlkreis*.
3. Wroth, British Museum Catalogue, *Imp. Byz. Coins*, p. 1, note, calls it a reel border, but this term is better kept for the distinct bobbin-shaped element in the Seleucid bead and reel border.
4. British Museum Catalogue, *Lycia*, pl. V, no. 8.
5. British Museum Catalogue, *Imp. Byz. Coins*, pl. XXV, no. 11.
6. Regling, *Sammlung Warren*, no. 92.
7. British Museum Catalogue, *Imp. Byz. Coins*, pl. XLVI, no. 2.

but there are bold examples in early times, as at Tarentum. [1] Combinations of pearled and plain circles are sometimes found : one of each on a coin of Cumae, [2] or a pearled one between two plain on many coins of the early South Italian fabric, as at Sybaris, Zancle, Metapontum ; indeed, at the latter mint this fashion is found outlasting the archaic period. [3] It is also found on a tenth century Byzantine coin. [4] These examples from Byzantine times have been mentioned because it is curious to note how the Byzantine coin-engravers, in their search for decorative detail, picked up certain elements which the Greeks had used and discarded at an early date. One pretty modification they invented for themselves ; along the middle of the three concentric pearled circles they placed larger pearls at intervals. [5]

The twisted plaited border which is variously described as cable or guilloche (pl. XXXVII, nos. 1, 2), is common on the earliest Magna-Graecian coinage, [6] elsewhere it is excessively rare. On the reverses of the Magna-Graecian coins with this ornament a border of radiating dashes usually takes the place of the cable, although sometimes the cable is repeated on the reverse. The dashes are sometimes arranged on either side of a plain circle so as to give a herring-bone pattern. [7]

As already stated, all these fancy borders passed out of use in the fine period of Greek coinage. But in the Hellenistic period, in Syria, there was invented what is known as the bead and reel, or fillet-border, which had a great vogue (e. g. pl. XVII, no. 1). The origin of this border is clear. [8] It is a kind of cord of wool, with knots at intervals, between which the soft wool fills out into the shape of a bead ; a net, called the agrenon, made of such cords, covered the omphalos on which Apollo is often represented seated (pl. XLIII, no. 4). The fillet which surrounds the head of the Seleucid kings on their coins thus carried an allusion to the god who protected them. This border was introduced by Antiochus III, the Great (222-187 B. C.). It continued in use, though not to the entire exclusion of the pearled border, on the obverse of Seleucid coins down to the end

1. Head, *Guide*, pl. 7, no. 5.
2. *Ibid.*, pl. 7, no. 2. So too a pearled and plain line along the edges of the incuse square, at Scepsis (*ibid.*, pl. 10, no. 26).
3. *Ibid.*, pl. 15, no. 6. Row of pearls between two straight lines, along the edges of the incuse square, at Methymna, *ibid.*, pl. 11, n° 27.
4. British Museum Catalogue, *Imp. Byz. Coins*, pl. LIII, no. 6.
5. British Museum Catalogue, *Imp. Byz. Coins*, pl. LIII, no. 15. It is interesting to find this motive (applied however to a single circle) used by an Italian medallist about 1500. He also uses the border of very flat beads, giving the effect of wire coiled round a hoop, on the same work (Brit. Mus., *Select Italian Medals*, pl. 37, no 5).
6. See Gabrici in *Atti del Congresso int. di sci. stor.*, Roma, 1903, vol. VI, p. 66 for the designs of these borders.
7. Babelon, *Traité*, pl. LXVIII, nos. 12ff. (Poseidonia) ; LXVII, nos. 2-4 (Siris and Pyxus).
8. Babelon, *Rois de Syrie*, p. lxxvi f ; quoting Cavedoni.

of the Empire under Tigranes the Armenian (pl. XVIII, no. 2). On other regal coins it is very scarce, being occasionally found on the Parthian and Bactrian series (Pl. XVII, no. 2). We also find it borrowed, for instance, by the Phoenician city of Tripolis, to surround the heads of the Dioscuri on the obverse of its tetradrachms. It has been remarked that on the later coins the real significance of the border seems to have been forgotten, for its true form is modified so as to resemble a well-known architectural moulding. On the barbarous coins of the Himyarites of S. Arabia the transformation goes still further, and the border appears to be made up of small vases. [1]

The adaptation of some portion or adjunct of the type for use as a border naturally suggested itself to the Greeks. It is hardly necessary to mention the dolphins on Syracusan coins, the grains of corn at Leontini, the fishes at Gela. At Camarina, where the subject is a water-nymph riding on a swan, we find a border of wave-pattern ; [2] at Heraclea in Lucania the edge of the aegis against which the head of Athena is seen forms an engrailed border ; [3] at Tarsus the god Baal-Tars sits within a circle of battlements, representing the enceinte of the city which he protects ; [4] at the Ionian Magnesia the conventional Maeander pattern surrounding the type alludes to the river on which the city lay. [5] It was also an obvious resource to arrange the inscription so as to border the design, as we have already noted (above, p. 15). One of the finest examples of the use of simple elements in perfect proportion is the design at Amphipolis (pl. LXIV, no. 4), where we find the inscription arranged along a plain square frame, slightly bevelled inwards. This use of inscriptions strung out along the sides of a square, one side of which is however sometimes wholly or partially occupied by a symbol, is characteristic of Macedon and Thrace.

The value of the wreath for bordering purposes was also not likely to escape the notice of the Greeks. In both the free and the conventional treatment they produced masterpieces. Of the former, admirable examples are found at Terina (pl. XXIX, no. 4) and Elis. [6] The coins of Mithradates the Great, on the other hand, and the Cistophori, show that the Greeks could make a border as ugly and lumbering as any one. [7]

The placing of the type on a shield — a natural thing to do, seeing that the coin-type

1. British Museum Catalogue, *Arabia*, etc., pl. VIII.
2. Head, *Guide*, pl. 16, no. 18.
3. *Ibid.*, pl. 24, no. 11.
4. British Museum Catalogue, *Lycaonia*, etc., pl. XXIX, nos. 11-15.
5. British Museum Catalogue, *Ionia*, pl. XVIII, nos. 1ff.
6. Head, *Guide*, pl. 14, no. 30.
7. *Ibid.*, pl. 60, nos. 2, 4, 5.

was in origin a kind of heraldic emblem — was not so common on Greek coins as one might expect. [1] But on the later coins of Macedon we find under Antigonus Gonatas (277-239 B. C.), Philip V (220-178 B. C.), and in the early days of the Roman dominion that the main type of the obverse, whether a head of Pan, of Perseus, or of Artemis, is placed in the centre of a Macedonian shield ; the type is so large in proportion that the remainder of the shield has the effect of a not very successful decorative border, rather than an organic part of the object. [2]

The questions with which we have been so far concerned are mostly external to the deeper problems of art ; they are questions of technique and decoration, not of meaning. What, if anything, do the coins reveal to us of the attitude of the ancients towards the significance of artistic representation ? Broadly speaking, we may be assured that no ancient artist had any inkling of the theory that art, so far as it was not mere pleasant decorative pattern, need be anything but direct 'imitation' of nature. Likeness was what was aimed at ; this was equally true of the artists of what is known as the period of finest art and of those of its most degraded or most conventional stages, however unequal may have been the measure of their attaiment.

Monumental remains, being so scanty, and so much more under the influence of tradition, in regard to the subjects represented, than the minor arts, can give us but a one-sided idea of the Greek artistic achievement. The eyes of students have been blinded by the too exclusive study of Greek sculpture [3] — slightly but inadequately corrected by a superficial acquaintance with Attic vase-painting — to the extraordinary fertility of imagination, delicacy and charm of conception, and variety of outlook on life that was characteristic of the Greeks.

The subject is one for a book, not for a part of a chapter. But let us consider one or two of the main points. First, the Greek idea of the gods. If we take the finest coin-types of the mainland, such as the Zeus and Hera of Olympia (pl. IV, no. 1, XXXIII, no. 1), or the Demeter of Anthela (pl. XXXV, no. 3), we find nothing out of keeping with the ideas which we may have learned from sculpture ; they are thoroughly ade-

1. E. g. Elis (Head, *Guide*, pl. 14, no. 33) ; Chios (Mavrogordato, *Coins of Chios*, pl. III) ; Lycia (British Museum Catalogue, *Lycia*, pl. VI, nos. 3, 16, pl. VII, nos. 7, 8, 10). On the so-called Wappenmünzen (Seltman, *Athens*, pl. I, II) the shield, if such it is, is not modelled but merely indicated by a linear circle.

2. Head, *Guide*, pl. 41, nos. 5, 7, pl. 54, nos. 10-12.

3. In something of the same way our ideas of the art of the Egyptians have been grievously distorted by the colossal statues and mummy cases which have been allowed to represent it to our eyes, to the exclusion of the miraculous achievements of their ' minor ' artists.

quate, dignified renderings of the Olympians. The influence of monumental religious sculpture is manifest. But in parts more removed from the great Sanctuaries of Greece, the atmosphere is very different. In Sicily, for instance, the heads of Apollo or of local nymphs are merely joyous representations of mortal youths and maidens, of which the essential quality is that they are fresh and full of life (pl. I, nos. 3, 4, II, 5, IV, 4, and all the series of Syracuse). There is none of that cold aloofness from mortal affairs which it has always been the custom to consider as characteristic of the Greek ideal of the gods. The fact is that the Sicilian engraver did not trouble himself about an ideal. What he gives us is an entirely fresh, unsophisticated rendering of a young and charming model, very much alive. The dignity which is inherent in all Greek art before the Hellenistic period prevents such renderings from being trivial. That epithet cannot be applied even to types like that of Terina, which represents a winged nymph or goddess playing with a bird (pl. XL, no. 2). But it must not be supposed that these artists took no thought of the character of the god whom they were representing. The corrective to such a misapprehension is supplied by such a type as the Dionysus of Naxos (pl. I, no. 2 and II, no. 1). Whether in the earlier form, which shows him sleek, well-groomed, self-indulgent, sneering and self-sufficient, or in the later, in which the character has been emasculated, we have a quite masterly presentation of the wine-god. The coins of another area — the coasts of Thrace and Macedon — betray, as a rule, a severer strain. It is true that the Apollo of Amphipolis (on coins of about 400 B. C.) is usually of a somewhat effeminate type (pl. VI, no. 1), but some of the more or less contemporary coins of the Chalcidian League (pl. III, nos. 1, 2) show the god at his noblest. Masculine enough, too, if not very intellectual, is the Hermes of Aenus (pl. II, no. 4, V, no. 2). All these heads present a remarkable contrast to the ideal which was favoured by most of the artists of Asia Minor about the same time. The Apollo on the unique coin of Old Smyrna is severe ; [1] but the emotional element in the Ionian character comes out well in the Apollo of Clazomenae and the Helios of Rhodes (pl. V, nos. 3-5), remarkable studies of passionate, sensuous types.

And what of the Greek attitude to the world of nature ? Strange statements are to be met with in books on Greek art about the lack of interest of Greek artists in nature and animal-life. Not to mention the eagle's head of Olympia (pl. LVII, no. 4) — perhaps the most masterly rendering of the subject in the whole of art, — a glance at the coins of Sicily and Southern Italy alone would serve to correct such absurd blunders.

1. Regling, *Die Münze als Kunstwerk*, pl. XXX, no. 646.

The world-famous eagles on the coins of Agrigentum (pl. LVIII, nos. 1, 2), the stag on coins of Caulonia (pl. LVI, no. 4), or the bull of Thurium (pl. LV, nos. 1, 3), have never been surpassed for keen observation and sympathetic treatment of animal form. The Sicilian engravers, as a matter of fact, took as much delight in naturalistic details which they were permitted to introduce into their designs as any Flemish illuminator of manuscripts, and they introduced them with more intelligence and relevance : the scarabaeus-beetle at Aetna (pl. I, no. 1), the sea-perch at Agrigentum, [1] the marsh-bird at Selinus (pl. XXXIX, no. 3) all have their significance. The Ionian artist, on the other hand, perhaps because of the Oriental tinge in him, is more brilliant as a decorator than as a naturalist. He is at his best in such a subject as the Chian sphinx (pl. LX, no. 1) or the Teian griffin (pl. LXI, no. 3), and when he does a bull, as at Samos, he is thinking more of its effect as decoration than of the force and majesty of the beast (pl. LV, no. 2).

It was not, however, always nature that inspired the coin-engraver ; he was also subject to the influence of other arts. It is true that we can trace but few deliberate copies of sculpture before the Hellenistic age ; when we do find such copies, they are usually of cultus-figures, such as the primitive stock of Hermes at Aenus. But the great statues more or less unconsciously influenced those who were familiar with them, and the various heads of Aphrodite on the coins of Cnidus from the middle of the fourth century onwards certainly betray, in different degrees, familiarity with the masterpiece of Praxiteles (pl. XXXI, no. 3, XXXVI, no. 2). Of actual copies we cannot speak here ; but we may give one example of the way in which certain coin-types betray inspiration. It comes from the Cretan city of Phaestus, where a series of coins, hardly later than the end of the fourth century, represent some of the labours of Heracles. [2] We find him standing between the apple-tree of the Hesperides and a huge rearing serpent ; fighting the serpent ; seizing one of the heads of the hydra and preparing to smash it with his club, while the crab attacks one of his feet (pl. XLIII, no. 1) ; and seated resting after his labours. Strangely enough, the contest with the Cretan bull is absent from the series. The hydra scene is treated with great freedom, the demigod being seen from behind ; but even more remarkable is the resting scene, in which the figure exactly anticipates the pose of the bronze statue of a pugilist in the Museo Nazionale at Rome — a work of considerably later date. The general impression created by this group of types is that they are not the invention of the die-engraver, but that they have been inspired

1. Hill, *Ancient Sicily*, pl. VII, no. 16.
2. British Museum Catalogue, *Crete*, pl. XV.

by some monumental series — in sculpture or painting — which was before his eyes.

The coins of Crete, indeed, stand out from among other Greek coins in virtue of a quality of picturesqueness combined with a narrative element, while, in regard to the subjects represented, they give hints of a somewhat mysterious background of myth and religion unlike anything that we find in other parts of Greece. The coins of Phaestus show us Europa seated, greeting Zeus, who, in the guise of a bull, comes out of the sea ; [1] or the youthful Zeus Welchanos (pl. XLIII, no. 2) seated among the branches of his sacred tree, holding one or two fighting cocks (symbols of ephebic beauty) ; or the winged demon Talos, [2] the brazen monster who, accompanied by his dog and armed with a stone, opposed the landing of the Argonauts. At Gortyna we see a female figure, Europa or Britomartis, seated pensive in a tree (pl. XLIII, no. 3), or embraced by the eagle. [3] Other types, more or less obscure, introduce us to a little known realm of religion ; but the point that concerns us here is that the artist shows a picturesque originality of treatment which indicates the existence of a school of art about which the monumental remains of Crete are altogether silent. One feels that, though a thousand years may have passed since the great times of the Minoan civilization, something has survived of the spirit of that culture.

The artist's attitude toward his subject may be studied in detail in another series of types ; to wit, the portraits of human beings. The reasons which so long excluded undisguised portraits of living persons from Greek coins were simple enough. The coin-type, as we have seen, was in origin a signet ; if a city chose for its coins a certain design, it was because that was its badge, by which its authority was recognized. Very frequently such a design happened to be the head or figure of a deity. No head or figure of a living mortal could serve such a purpose. Hence the only heads that appeared on early coins were those of deities ; and for a ruler to put his own portrait on his coins would have laid him open to the charge of posing as a god. It was not until Oriental nfluence familiarized the Greeks with the idea of king-worship that the old prejudice was broken down. The gradual process, and the exceptions to the rule that may be detected, cannot be discussed here, where we are rather concerned with the technique of portraiture and with the method of rendering likeness. It has already been hinted that the heads of deities on certain Sicilian coins are no other than portraits of models,

1. British Museum Catalogue, *Crete*, pl. XIV, no. 16.
2. *Ibid.*, pl. XV, no. 11 ; XVI, no. 6.
3. *Ibid.*, pl. IX, no. 5, to X, no. 8.

fitted with certain attributes, such as a laurel-wreath for Apollo, leaves of a water-plant for Arethusa. But undisguised portraits first appear in Asia Minor towards the end of the fifth century. Most of them represent not pure Greeks, but Orientals. We have satraps such as Pharnabazus [1] or Tissaphernes, the latter (pl. VII, no. 3) a very dignified rendering of a fine aristocratic Oriental type. Or we have the princelings who ruled in Lycia, very characteristic heads, heavy-nosed, thick-lipped, luxuriantly bearded. On the other hand, of the one or two Greek portraits on coins of the time, the best known is a startlingly realistic head of a man on a stater of Cyzicus, with rugged, almost grotesque features (pl. VII, no. 5). [2] It comes as a shock to those who do not understand that even about 400 B. C. there was such a thing as realistic portraiture. Lucian describes the portrait of the Corinthian general Pelichos by Demetrius of Alopeke thus : with projecting paunch and bald head, half nude, a few stray hairs of his beard blown about by the wind, his veins standing out on the flesh, the very man himself. We know that certain sculptural types of Athens were reproduced on Cyzicene coins. May it be that this weirdly realistic head is a copy of some sculptured portrait of the school of Demetrius ?

But this excessive realism is not characteristic of coins of the time. In fact, intentional coin-portraits of any kind may be counted on the fingers of one hand until we reach the third century. At this time the tendency to lay stress on individual physical peculiarities was beginning to show itself in official portraiture ; we know, for instance, that certain features, such as the inclination of the head to one side, or a peculiar rising lock of hair above the forehead, were among the marks by which Alexander the Great was distinguished in official portraits. But pure realism had not quite broken down the old reserve. The coin-portraits of Seleucus I (pl. X, no. 2), of Demetrius Poliorcetes (pl. IX, no. 5) of Hiero II of Syracuse (pl. XI, no. 2), of Diodotus of Bactria (pl. XII, no. 4) all have, first of all, dignity and all aim at a certain ideal quality. The portraits of Antiochus I of Syria, and of Philetaerus of Pergamum, on the other hand, show in this period the beginnings of the purely realistic style ; the artist, so far as we can judge, has not thought of idealising his subjects. The portrait of Antiochus (pl. X, no. 3) is a masterly study of a shrewd old warrior. As to the eunuch Philetaerus (pl. XI, no. 1), his peculiar facial developement is most faithfully rendered, and withal the artist gives

---

1. Hill, *Historical Greek Coins*, no. 30 ; Babelon, pl. CLXXVIII, no. 15.
2. There are at least two other remarkable portrait-heads on Cyzicene staters of about the same time ; all three are shown in *Nomisma*, vii, 1912, pl. VI, nos. 9, 10, 11.

vivid expression to the cynical pride of the man whose astuteness enabled him to triumph over his physical disability.

Towards the end of the third century the realistic method is triumphantly established. Two of the most remarkable portraits in the whole range of art represent kings of Pontus : Mithradates II (240-190 B. C.) and his successor Pharnaces (190-169 B. C.). Was there ever a more wonderful study of a semi-barbarian than the portrait of Pharnaces (pl. XIV, no. 1) ? Note the excessive development of the lower part of the face, the heavy cheeks, the almost negroid lips, combined with the sensitive nostrils. Observe the contrast with the comparatively small occiput. The conical shape of the head may perhaps be due to that artificial compression in infancy which it is recorded was practised by some of the Pontic races. All these features are noticeable, but in a less developed form, in his predecessor Mithradates (pl. XIII, no. 2). But the artist gets deeper than mere external features ; his treatment of brow and eye has given just that expression of melancholy which is often perceptible in the face of the intelligent bar-barian, as in the faces of the more intelligent animals. The nearest parallel to it is per-haps the wonderful portrait of a man wearing a fez on a Syriam garnet, formerly in the Tyszkiewicz collection, afterwards at Lewes House. [1] It has something of the same quality of melancholy. Not far removed in date from the coin of Pharnaces but perhaps a little earlier — about 200 — is the famous coin of Antimachus, a Greek who ruled over Bactria and N. W. India (pl. XVI, no. 2). At first very attractive, it is by no means so fine a work of art as the Pharnaces. The detail is poor ; note the careless rendering of the hair and the cloak. Poorness of design and workmanship are also seen in the reverse : a certain test of the artist's real powers. But it is, when all is said, a clever study, reminding one of some Italian condottiere of the Renaissance. It is wonderful to think that such coins were produced in what is now Turkestan, and fascinating to look forward to the treasures of sculpture that may be revealed when Balkh comes under the spade of the excavator.

Throughout this period the level of portraiture remains very high, from the techni-cal point of view. It is in the reverse types that we find out the artist's weakness. The rare coin of Orophernes of Cappadocia (pl. XV, no. 2), struck in the year 158-7, was probably the work of some Ionian artist. Here again the design of the reverse is poor ; but how admirably refined and aristocratic, how gentlemanly, in fact, the

1. J. D. Beazley, *The Lewes House Collection of Ancient Gems*, pl. 6, no. 97.

portrait of the king ! This kind of respectability, in periods when art is not inspired by the highest ideals, goes side by side with brutal realism. Almost contemporary with Orophernes was Heliocles of Greek India (pl. XVII, no. 2). It is an uncompromising portrait, the very likeness of a peppery colonel, such as one may see in the pages of English comic papers.

As time progresses, good workmanship and dignity of conception become more rare. Yet one of the most brilliant of all Greek portraits represents Mithradates the Great (pl. XVIII, no. 1). Ruskin has devoted some lines of severe criticism to this coin. He speaks of it sarcastically as showing what we moderns call " vigour of character; " he describes the features as finished with great care and subtlety, but at the cost of simplicity and breadth. He also finds fault with its disorder in design ; and complains that the locks of hair cannot be counted any longer — they are entirely dishevelled and irregular. The licentiousness, the casting loose of the masses in the design, is, he says, an infallible sign of the decline of art. He goes on to describe the manifold crimes of which Mithradates was guilty, and argues that it could not have been beneficial to art that any attempt should have been made to study his portrait.

It would be difficult to find anywhere more bad criticism crowded into so short a space. The hair is dishevelled, but that is the artist's method of representing a passionate moment. The details are not so minutely finished as to obscure the breadth of design — breadth and simplicity of design are indeed characteristic of the face, and the modelling is superb. It cannot be denied that it shows the ethos of the man, his character. If he was subject to violent spasms of emotion, that tendency is indicated. But there is indicated at the same time a certain idealism. Probably it was somewhat theatrical ; but then it was a case of the theatrical pose becoming a second nature. Not a noble, tragic subject, suitable for a Polygnotus ; but at any rate hardly worse than many a ruler whose portraits were worth doing because they had character, good or bad. It is in works like this that the Greek conception approaches the Renaissance.

The subject of portraiture on Greek coins brings us naturally to the art of Roman coins, the chief attraction of which is admittedly the portraits which they bear. The engravers at the Roman mint or mints in the early days of the empire down to the period of the Flavians take a high position as portrait-artists. There are very few portraits produced in Greek lands under the Empire which can in any way compare with those on Roman coins. What was the nationality of the engravers employed by the Romans, we do not know ; but probably a large proportion of them, especially in the earlier period, were Greeks. One of the most characteristically Roman types of head, the portrait [1] of a Domitius Ahenobarbus, on an aureus commemorating the victory of Cn. Domitius Ahenobarbus over Domitius Calvinus off Brundisium in 42 B. C., must have been produced in Greece, since Cnaeus was of the party of the regicides. It is a masterpiece of realism. On the other hand a purely idealistic treatment of the features of Augustus is found on the beautiful aureus issued about 27 B. C., with a heifer as the reverse type (pl. XVIII, no 4) ; this also is Greek in origin. Very well composed also is the silver 'medallion' of Augustus of the same period, probably struck at Pergamum, which has as its reverse his signet-type of the sphinx, itself a finely decorative compos- ition (pl. XVIII, no. 3, LX, no. 4) ; but the weakness of technique is apparent in our enlargements.

In what has preceded, we have assumed that the development of the engraver's art is straightforward, whether it be in the direction of improvement or in that of degrada- tion. This may be true, as a general rule ; but it must not be forgotten that artists are subject to the temptation to imitate the manner of their predecessors, and that, conse- quently, we have sometimes to reckon with a 'throw-back' to an early style ; in other words with archaistic handling. When an artist of a comparatively late school is imitating the manner of one very much earlier, it is usually not very difficult to see what he is doing ; but when he is nearer in time to his model, detection is less easy. The classical instance of archaism in coins is provided by Athens. The tetradrachms which were issued in the fourth century, says Head [2], " are roughly engraved and carelessly struck. They are, in fact, only imitations of the older coins. The semblance of archaism is, however, delusive, as is evident from the manner in which the eye of the goddess is shown *in profile*. The die-engraver seems to have been trammelled by the condition imposed upon him of adhering to the old familiar types. He does not deliberately revert to archaism on aesthetic principles ; on the contrary, he is conscientiously trying to emancipate himself from the fixed hieratic type which he was set to copy, and he modernizes, as far as possible, the head of Athena, without venturing to depart from the general outlines of the older type. " This style of tetradrachm is supposed to have been inaugurated in 393 B. C. It is not difficult to distinguish from the coin of the fifth century, partly on account of the treatment of the eye, partly by the rough work- manship. But these coins are not the first case of archaizing at the Athenian mint.

1. Head, *Guide*, pl. 66, no. 20.
2. *Historia Numorum*, 2nd. ed., p. 374.

From the years immediately following the Persian Wars down to the close of the
century the change in style is hardly perceptible, and it is almost impossible to make a
chronological arrangement of the issues. Everything about the older coins is most
carefully reproduced in the later. The issues have, indeed, been divided into " good
archaic work " (pl. XX, no. 2), " good later archaic work, " and " rough archaic work, "
but there must always remain a number of individual specimens of which the classi-
fication is doubtful. The motive for this archaistic treatment is supposed to have been
economic ; it is thought that the wide currency which the Attic silver enjoyed made
it undesirable to modernize its style ; barbarians, especially, are apt to reject new coins
if they diverge in the least particular from the model to which they are accustomed.
Certainly no other explanation of the strange history of the Attic coinage has been
proposed. The theory is confirmed by the fact that no other of the great early currencies,
such as the Corinthian or Aeginetic, was popular among the barbarians.

It is clear, on any hypothesis, that the archaism of the Athenian coins was dictated
by some non-aesthetic motive ; it is not in the same case with the English " Gothic
florin " but rather with the Florentine florin or the Venetian ducat, the types of which
remained immobilized for centuries, although their style changed perceptibly.

Archaism is seldom so easy to detect as in these Athenian coins. It is often difficult to know whether the artist is merely backward and old-fashioned, or really deliberately archaizing. And we must, of course, rule out those cases in which an engraver
is copying some archaic or archaistic type of statue, such as the fighting Athena on
the coins of Ptolemy Soter (Pl. XLIV, no. 2). A certain example is however found at
Hyria in Campania, where, on coins of the fourth century B. C., we see the profile head
of Athena with such a detail as the eye treated in the archaic manner. [1] And there can
be no doubt about the archaizing treatment of the Pegasus on certain coins of Corinth
of the fourth century, where he is represented with the curled wing properly characteristic of a much earlier period. Observe however that other details, and the modelling
generally, are not archaic in treatment. On the whole, it may be said that archaism in
style is an exceptional thing in Greek coins, so far as we can detect it.

If the ancient coin-engravers sometimes copied the style of their predecessors, they
also, in a degree which is more frequently discernible, copied their contemporaries.
Here we must distinguish motives. Sometimes the object in view was purely commer-

1. *Numismatic Chronicle*, 1921, p. 163.

cial. The authorities at one mint imitated the products of another because they had a good reputation, with the hope that their own coins would pass current in the same way ; thus the barbarians of Southern Arabia imitated the Athenian coins. Sometimes the reason may have been merely a lack of originality on the part of the imitators ; this we may assume as the explanation of the imitations of Syracusan and other Greek coins by the Phoenicians in Sicily. An impudent example of this kind is a didrachm struck by the Solontines in exact imitation of one of Selinus, with Heracles fighting the bull on the obverse, and on the reverse a river-god sacrificing ; even the peculiar symbol of Selinus, the selinon-leaf, is reproduced. [1] A third reason may have been some political relation between the two states. Thus a colony, like Abdera, would reproduce the types of its mother-city, Teos (compare pl. LXI, nos. 2 and 3), or the colonies of Corinth would imitate the Corinthian " pegasi ".

The kind of imitation, however, with which we are properly concerned here is that which was inspired by admiration for the beauty of the type, not for its commercial convenience. The best example has already been mentioned ; the facing head of the nymph Arethusa by Kimon on the coins of Syracuse was copied with some exactitude at Larisa in Thessaly on coins of the early fourth century (pl. XXXI, no. 4) and, with much less skill, at Tarsus in Cilicia on coins issued by Pharnabazus in the period 379-374 B. C., and also at other places. Tarsus again, about the middle of the fourth century, copies from the gold coins of Syracuse the group of Heracles strangling the lion. Other interesting examples, in which Syracuse again affords the model, are provided by the coinage of the Opuntian Locrians and of the Aetolians. The early fourth century coins of Opus (pl. XXXIV, no. 1) have on the obverse a head of a goddess crowned with leaves, so exactly resembling the head of Arethusa by Euaenetus, and on the reverse a figure of the Locrian Ajax (pl. XLIII, no. 5) so closely modelled on that of the Syracusan hero Leukaspis, that it has been suggested that this is not an instance of copying, but that " these types were designed for the Opuntians at the Syracusan mint, and that the dies (for the first issue at any rate) were executed there. " However this may be, the motive was one and the same. It would be easy to multiply instances of such imitations, and we must be content with mentioning but one more. The citizens of Chersonesus in Crete evidently admired the coins of Stymphalus in Arcadia, for the head of Britomartis on their fourth century staters is modelled on the head of the

1. Hill, *Coins of Ancient Sicily*, pl. VI, no. 14 compared with pl. VI, no. 6.

Stymphalian Artemis (pl. XXXIV, no. 2), and they also copied the reverse type of the Arcadian city, Heracles striking with uplifted club (pl. XLII, no. 6). Examples of the coinage of Chersonesus which have any claim to be works of art are excessively rare ; the great majority are very rude, not to say barbarous, copies. If we compare the finer specimens with the Stymphalian staters we shall see that here, at least, it is not a case of ordering dies from the artist who engraved the coins which took the fancy of the Chersonesians. Their coins are copies, lacking something of the life of the original. Yet it is clear, from the rapid falling away in style of the later Chersonesian issues, that there was no engraver permanently in Chersonesus itself capable of making such a copy. Some artist in some other city must have been given a specimen of the coin of Stymphalus and told to do his best. Many other series in Crete show the same fairly good beginning and a rapid collapse in style. It seems certain that the authorities of these places thought, as so many other town-councils have thought after them, that all that was necessary, in order to obtain a good civic design, was to find a good model and set local talent to work on imitating it

DESCRIPTION OF THE PLATES

DESCRIPTION OF THE PLATES

PLATE I.

1. CATANA (Sicily) under the name of Aetna. Head of bald Silenus, wreathed with ivy ; below, scarabaeus beetle. Inscription *Aitnaion*. (For reverse, see pl. XXXVIII, n° 2.) 476-461. Silver tetradrachm. Royal Library, Brussels.

2. NAXOS (Sicily). Head of Dionysus, wreathed with ivy. About 460. (For reverse, see pl. XXXVIII, no. 1.) Silver tetradrachm.

3. LEONTINI (Sicily). Head of Apollo, wreathed with laurel. (For reverse, see pl. LIII, no. 2.) About 450. Silver tetradrachm.

4. CATANA (Sicily). Head of Apollo, wreathed with laurel ; behind, a fish. Inscription *Katanaion*. About 450. Silver tetradrachm. Mr. W. H. Woodward.

PLATE II.

1. NAXOS (Sicily). Head of Dionysus, wearing metal fillet decorated with ivy. (For reverse, see Pl. XL no. 2.) About 450-440. Silver tetradrachm.

2. CAMARINA (Sicily). Head of young Heracles wearing lion-skin ; in front, spray of olive. Inscription *Kamarinaion*. About 450. Silver tetradrachm.

3. MYTILENE (Lesbos). Head of Apollo wreathed with laurel. Inscription *Myti*. About 440-400. Electrum stater.

4. AENUS (Thrace). Head of Hermes wearing petasus. About 440-412. Silver tetradrachm. Capt. E. G. Spencer-Churchill.

5. CATANA (Sicily). Head of Apollo wreathed with laurel ; behind, laurel leaf and berry. Inscription *Katanaion*. About 430. Silver tetradrachm. M. R. Jameson.

PLATE III.

1. CHALCIDICE (Macedon). Head of Apollo to left, wreathed with laurel. About 392-358. Silver tetradrachm.

2. CHALCIDICE (Macedon). Similar to no. 1, but to right. About 392-358. Silver tetra-drachm.

3. MARONEA (Thrace). Head of young Dionysus wreathed with ivy. About 415-400. Silver tetradrachm.

4. GELA (Sicily). Head of river-god Gelas, horned, surrounded by three fish. (Reverse of pl. L, no. 2). About 415-405. Silver tetradrachm. Royal Library, Brussels.

PLATE IV.

1. OLYMPIA (Elis). Head of Zeus, laureate. About 421-365. Silver stater.

2. THASOS (island off Thrace). Head of Dionysus, wreathed with ivy. (For reverse, see Pl. XL, no. 4.) About 411-390. Silver tetradrachm. Capt. E. G. Spencer-Churchill.

3. RHEGIUM (Bruttium). Head of Apollo, wreathed with laurel. About 415-387. Silver tetradrachm.

4. CATANA (Sicily) by Euaenetus. Head of Apollo, wreathed with laurel ; behind, crayfish ; in front, bell on a cord. (For obverse, see pl. L, no. 3.) About 413-404. Silver tetradrachm. Private Collection.

PLATE V.

1. CATANA (Sicily) by Herakleidas. Head of Apollo wreathed with laurel. On the left, signature *Herakleida*. About 413-404. Silver tetradrachm.

2. AENUS (Thrace). Head of Hermes wearing petasus. (For reverse, see pl. LVI, no. 2.) About 412-365. Silver tetradrachm. Capt. E. G. Spencer-Churchill.

3. RHODES. Head of the Sun-god. (For reverse, see pl. LXII, no. 3.) About 400-333. Gold stater.

4. CLAZOMENAE (Ionia). Head of Apollo, wreathed with laurel. (For reverse, see pl. LVIII no. 3.) About 387-300. Silver tetradrachm.

5. RHODES. Head of the Sun-god. (For reverse, see pl. LXII, no. 4.) About 400-333. Silver tetradrachm.

PLATE VI.

1. AMPHIPOLIS (Macedon). Head of Apollo, wreathed with laurel. (For reverse, see pl. LXIV, no. 4.) About 424-358. Silver tetradrachm.

2. CYRENE (N. Africa). Head of Zeus Ammon, with ram's horns, wreathed with laurel, surrounded by laurel-wreath. About 400. Silver tetradrachm.

3. SYBRITA (Crete). Head of Dionysus, wreathed with ivy ; in front, a bunch of grapes. (For obverse, see no. 4.) About 350 B. C. Silver stater.

4. SYBRITA (Crete). Head of Hermes, wearing flat petasus ; in front, his caduceus. Inscription *Sybrition*. (Reverse of no. 3.) About 350 B. C. Silver stater.

PLATE VII.

1. Lampsacus (Mysia). Head of Actaeon, stag's horn sprouting from forehead. About 394-350. Gold stater.

2. LAMPSACUS (Mysia). Head of Dionysus, wreathed with ivy. About 394-350. Gold stater.

3. TISSAPHERNES, Persian satrap, in Caria(?). Portrait-head, in satrapal headdress (kyrbasia). (For reverse, see pl. LXIV, no. 2.) About 395. Silver tetradrachm.

4. CYZICUS (Mysia). Bearded head in conical cap wreathed with laurel, perhaps a Kabeiros ; below, a tunny-fish. About 410-334. Electrum Stater.

5. CYZICUS (Mysia). Bearded realistic portrait-head, wreathed with laurel ; below, a tunny-fish. About 410-334. Electrum Stater.

PLATE VIII.

1. CYRENE (N. Africa). Head of Zeus Ammon, with ram's horn at temple. Behind, spray of laurel. About 390. Silver tetradrachm.

2. ARCADIAN FEDERATION. Head of Lycaean Zeus, laureate. About 370-362. Silver tetradrachm.

3. PHILIP II, king of Macedon. Head of Apollo, laureate. 359-336. Gold stater.

4. PANTICAPAEUM (Crimea). Head of bearded satyr, with pointed ears. (For reverse, see pl. LXI, no. 9.) About 350. Gold stater.

5. OLYMPIA (Elis). Head of Zeus laureate. Inscription *Waleion*. About 363-343. Silver tetradrachm.

6. PHILIP II, king of Macedon. Head of Zeus, laureate. 395-336. Silver tetradrachm.

PLATE IX.

1. ALEXANDER the Great. Head of Heracles in lion-skin. Struck in Cyprus. After about 325. Silver tetradrachm.

2. LYSIMACHUS, king of Thrace. Head of Alexander the Great, with ram's horn at temple, diademed. (For reverse, compare pl. XLIV, no. 1.) 323-281. Silver tetradrachm.

3. ALEXANDER son of Neoptolemus, king of Epirus. Head of Zeus, laureate. (For reverse, see pl. LXIII, no. 4.) 342-326. Gold stater.

4. PTOLEMY I, Soter, king of Egypt. Head of Alexander the Great, in elephant-skin. 323-305. Silver tetradrachm.

5. DEMETRIUS POLIORCETES, king of Macedon. His portrait, with bull's horn, diademed. (For reverse, compare pl. XLV, no. 1.) 306-283. Silver tetradrachm.

PLATE X.

1. SELEUCUS I, Nicator, king of Syria. Head of Heracles, in lion-skin. (For reverse, see pl. XLV, no. 2.) 306-280. Silver tetradrachm.

2. PHILETAERUS, king of Pergamum (Mysia). Head of Seleucus I, diademed. 284-263. Silver tetradrachm.

3. ANTIOCHUS I, Soter, king of Syria. His portrait, diademed. 281-261. Silver tetradrachm.

4. PTOLEMY I, Soter, king of Egypt. His portrait, diademed, and wearing aegis. 305-285. Silver tetradrachm.

PLATE XI.

1. EUMENES I, king of Pergamum. Head of the eunuch Philetaerus, wearing diadem and laurel-wreath entwined. 263-241. Silver tetradrachm.

2. HIERO II, king of Syracuse. His portrait, diademed. 269-216. Silver thirty-two litrae.

PLATE XII.

1. BAGADAT I, king of Persis. His portrait, wearing eastern head-dress (kyrbasia), diademed. About 250. Silver tetradrachm.

2. SELEUCUS II, Callinicus, king of Syria. His portrait, diademed. 246-226. Silver tetradrachm.

3. ANTIOCHUS HIERAX, king of Asia Minor (?). His portrait, diademed. 246-227. Silver tetradrachm.

4. DIODOTUS, king of Bactria. His portrait, diademed. (For reverse, see pl. XLVI, no. 1.) About 250. Gold stater.

PLATE XIII.

1. AETOLIAN LEAGUE. Head of Demetrius Aetolicus, son of Antigonus Gonatas (?), wearing wreath entwined with diadem. (For reverse, compare pl. XLVI, no. 2.) About 235-233. Silver stater.

2. MITHRADATES III, king of Pontus. His portrait, diademed. About 220-185. Silver tetradrachm.

3. PHILIP V, king of Macedon. His portrait, diademed. 220-179. Silver tetradrachm.

PLATE XIV.

1. PHARNACES 1, king of Pontus. His portrait, diademed. About 185-169. Silver tetradrachm.

2. PERSEUS, king of Macedon. His portrait, diademed, 178-168. Silver tetradrachm.

PLATE XV.

1. EUTHYDEMUS II, king of Bactria and India. His portrait, diademed. About 170-160. Silver tetradrachm.

2. OROPHERNES, king of Cappadocia. His portrait, diademed. 158-157. Struck at Priene in Ionia. Silver tetradrachm.

PLATE XVI.

1. DEMETRIUS I, Soter, king of Syria. His portrait, diademed. 162-150. Silver tetradrachm.

2. ANTIMACHUS, king of Bactria and India. His portrait, diademed, and wearing Macedonian kausia. About 150. Silver tetradrachm.

PLATE XVII.

1. ANTIOCHUS VI, Dionysus, king of Syria. His portrait, diademed and radiate. Fillet border. 145-142. Silver tetradrachm.

2. HELIOCLES, king of Bactria and India. His portrait, diademed. About 150-125. Silver tetradrachm.

PLATE XVIII.

1. MITHRADATES VI EUPATOR, the Great. His portrait, diademed. 76-75. Silver tetradrachm.

2. TIGRANES the Great, King of Armenia and Syria. His portrait, wearing Armenian tiara adorned with two eagles and a star. Struck at Antioch in Syria. 83-69. Silver tetradrachm.

3. AUGUSTUS. His portrait. Inscription : *Imperator Caesar*. (For reverse see pl. LX, no. 4.) Struck in Asia Minor (Pergamum ?). 27-20. Silver cistophorus.

4. AUGUSTUS. His portrait. Inscription : *Caesar*. Struck in the Eastern provinces. (For reverse, see pl. LVI, no. 5.) 27-20. Aureus.

PLATE XIX.

1. ATHENS. Head of Athena in crested helmet. About 527-510. Silver tetradrachm. Mr. J. I. S. Whitaker.

2. SYRACUSE. Female head, hair bound with fillet surrounded by dolphins. Inscription : *Syraqosion*. About 500-485. Silver tetradrachm.

3. SYRACUSE. Head of Arethusa, hair bound with pearled cord, surrounded by dolphins. Inscription : *Syrakosion*. About 400-485. Silver tetradrachm.

4. CORINTH. Head of Athena, helmeted. About 480. Silver stater.

PLATE XX.

1. SYRACUSE (the Demareteion). Head of Arethusa, wreathed with laurel, surrounded by dolphins. Inscription : *Syrakosion*. (Reverse of pl. XLIX, no. 4.) 480 Commemorating the defeat of the Carthaginians at Himera in 480. Silver decadrachm.

2. ATHENS. Head of Athena, in crested helmet adorned with olive-leaves. (For reverse, see pl. LVII no. 2.) About 470. Silver tetradrachm.

3. SYRACUSE. Head of Arethusa, hair bound with pearled cord, surrounded by dolphins. Inscription as before. About 478-470. Silver tetradrachm.

4. CNIDUS (Caria). Head of Aphrodite, hair bound with pearled cord. About 480. Silver drachm.

PLANCHE XXI.

1. SYRACUSE. Head of Arethusa, hair bound with pearled cord, surrounded by

dolphins. Inscription as before. About 470-460. Silver tetradrachm. Mr. A. H. Lloyd.

2. SYRACUSE. Head of Arethusa, hair bound three times with cord, surrounded by dolphins. Inscription as before. About 470-460. Silver tetradrachm.

3. SYRACUSE. Head of Arethusa, hair taken up behind and bound with broad band. Dolphins and inscription as before. About 470-460. Silver tetradrachm. Mr. A. H. Lloyd.

4. SYRACUSE. Head of Arethusa, hair taken up behind and bound with broad band. Dolphins and inscription as before. About 470-460. Silver tetradrachm. Mr. A. H. Lloyd.

PLATE XXII.

1. SYRACUSE. Head of Arethusa, hair drawn up and tied on crown. Dolphins and inscription as before. About 460-450. Silver tetradrachm.

2. SYRACUSE. Similar to preceding, with signature *A* behind neck. About 460-450. Silver tetradrachm. Mr. A. H. Lloyd.

3. SYRACUSE. Head of Arethusa, wreathed, hair in coif decorated with key-pattern. Dolphins and inscription as before. About 450. Silver tetradrachm.

4. SYRACUSE. Head of Arethusa, hair taken up and bound four times with cord. Dolphins and inscription as before. About 450. Silver tetradrachm.

PLATE XXIII.

1. SYRACUSE. Head of Arethusa, back hair in net, band with key pattern over forehead. Dolphins and inscription as before. About 450-440. Silver tetradrachm.

2. SYRACUSE, by Sosion. Head of Arethusa, signed on the head-band *Sosion*. Dolphins and inscription as before. About 425. Silver tetradrachm. University of Aberdeen.

3. SYRACUSE. Similar to preceding, but without signature. About 425. Silver tetradrachm.

4. THURIUM (Lucania). Head of Athena in crested helmet bound with olive. In front, artist's signature *Ph*. About 425. Silver stater.

PLATE XXIV.

1. SYRACUSE (by Euaenetus). Head of Arethusa, hair in sling decorated with stars at back, and dolphin over waves on forehead. Dolphins as before ; inscription *Syrakosion*, signature *Euai.* on the belly of the dolphin before the mouth. About 420-413. Silver tetradrachm. Mr. A. H. Lloyd.

2. SYRACUSE (by Eumenos). Head of Arethusa, signed on the head-band *Eumenou*. Dolphins and inscription as before. About 425. Silver tetradrachm.

3. SYRACUSE (by Eucleidas). Head of Arethusa ; before neck, tablet with the signature *Eukleida*. Dolphins and inscription as before. About 425-413. Silver tetradrachm.

4. SYRACUSE (by Phrygillus). Head of Arethusa, hair in sling, signature *Phry*. on the forehead-band. Dolphins and inscription as before. About 413-399. Silver tetradrachm.

PLATE XXV.

1. SYRACUSE. Head of Arethusa, bending forward, hair taken up and tied at back of crown. Dolphins as before. Inscription *Syrakosion*. About 413-399. Silver tetradrachm

2. SYRACUSE (by Eucleidas). Head of Athena in crested helmet, on which is the signature *Eukleida*. Dolphins and inscription as before. About 413-399. Silver tetradrachm.

3. SYRACUSE. Head of Persephone, with flowing hair, wreathed with barley. Dolphins and inscription as before. (Flaw in the die behind the head.) About 413-399. Silver tetradrachm.

4. SYRACUSE. Head of Arethusa, hair in sling adorned with stars. Dolphins and inscription as before. About 413-399. Silver tetradrachm. Mr. A. H. Lloyd.

PLATE XXVI.

1. SYRACUSE (by Kimon). Head of Arethusa, hair in net ; signature *Kim*. on the forehead-band. Dolphins and inscription as before. (For reverse, compare pl. LI, no. 1.) About 413-405. Silver decadrachm. Mr. C. S. Gulbenkian.

2. SYRACUSE (by Kimon). Head of Arethusa in higher relief, hair in net ; signature *K* on forehead-band. Dolphins and inscription as before ; on the dolphin below the neck, *Kimon*. About 413-405. Silver decadrachm.

PLATE XXVII.

1. SYRACUSE (by Kimon). Head of Arethusa ; on forehead-band signature *Kimon* ; dolphins playing among her hair ; outside the border, *Arethosa*. (For reverse, see Pl. L, no. 4.) About 413-399. Silver tetradrachm.

2. SYRACUSE. Head of Arethusa, hair in sling adorned with stars. Dolphins and signature as before. Unsigned, but probably by the artist who signs *Parme*., copying the artist of Pl. XXV, no. 2. About 413-399. Silver tetradrachm. Mr. A. H. Lloyd.

3. SYRACUSE. Head of Arethusa, bending forward, hair flying behind. Dolphins and inscription as before. About 399-387. Silver tetradrachm. Mr. A. H. Lloyd.

4. NEAPOLIS (Macedon). Head of the maiden-goddess of the city, laureate. Inscription. *Neop.* About 390. Silver drachm.

PLATE XXVIII.

1. SYRACUSE (by Euaenetus). Head of Arethusa crowned with water-plant. Dolphins and inscription as usual. Below lowest dolphin, signature *Euainetou.* About 413-400. Silver decadrachm. Formely in the Montagu Collection.

2. SYRACUSE (by an unknown artist). Head of Arethusa crowned with water-plant, Dolphins and inscription as before. Style more florid than no. 1. (For reverse, see pl. LII, no. 1.) About 400-390. Silver decadrachm.

PLATE XXIX.

1. SYRACUSE (by Euaenetus). Head of Arethusa, hair in sling adorned with stars. In front, inscription as usual ; behind, signature *Euai.* About 413-400. Gold hundred-litra piece. Mr. A. H. Lloyd.

2. SYRACUSE. Head of Arethusa and inscription as on no. 1 ; no signature ; behind head, a star. (For reverse, see pl. XLVII, no. 3.) About 413-400. Gold hundred-litra piece. Capt. E. G. Spencer-Churchill.

3. SEGESTA (Sicily). Head of the nymph Segesta, hair in sling adorned with stars ; behind, ear of barley ; in front, inscription *Segestazia.* About 415-409. Silver tetradrachm.

4. TERINA (Bruttium). Head of nymph Terina, head-band adorned with palmette ; behind, signature *Ph.* The whole in olive-wreath. (For reverse, see pl. XLI, no. 2.) About 425-400. Silver stater.

5. EUBOEA. Head of the nymph Euboea. About 411-378. Silver stater.

PLATE XXX.

1. METAPONTUM (Lucania). Head of nymph, hair bound twice with narrow riband. About 400. Silver stater.

2. METAPONTUM. Head of Homonoia (Concord). About 400. Silver stater.

3. METAPONTUM. Head of nymph, hair bound twice with narrow riband. About 400. Silver stater. Mr. A. H. Lloyd.

4. METAPONTUM. Head of nymph, in the manner of Kimon (cp. pl. XXVI, no. 2). About 400-375. Silver stater.

PLATE XXXI.

1. CARTHAGINIANS IN SICILY. Head of a queen (Dido ?) or Oriental goddess wearing Oriental head-dress, tied with diadem adorned with palmettes. (For reverse, see pl. LIII, no. 5.) About 400-370. Silver tetradrachm.

2. CARTHAGINIANS IN SICILY. Head of Persephone, crowned with barley (inspired by the decadrachm of Syracuse, pl. XXVIII, no. 1). About 400-370. Silver tetradrachm.

3. CNIDUS. Head of Aphrodite ; on the head-band signature, in monogram, *Sa* ; behind a prow (symbol of the goddess as giver of fair voyages). Traces of inscription, *Kni*. (For reverse, see pl. LIII, no. 4.) About 400-390. Silver tetradrachm.

4. LARISA (Thessaly). Head of nymph Larisa (inspired by Kimon's Arethusa, pl. XXVII, no. 5). About 400-350. Silver drachm.

PLATE XXXII.

1. THURIUM (Lucania). Head of Athena, in crested helmet, adorned with figure of Scylla. About 400-350. Silver distater.

2. VELIA (Lucania). Head of Athena, in crested helmet, adorned with a gryphon, Behind, signature *R*. About 390. Silver stater.

3. CORINTH. Head of Athena in helmet. Behind, palmette. About 390. Silver stater.

4. LAMPSACUS (Mysia). Head of Demeter, crowned with barley. About 390-350. Gold stater.

5. LAMPSACUS (Mysia). Head of winged Aphrodite, crowned with myrtle (?). About 390-350. Gold stater.

PLATE XXXIII.

1. OLYMPIA (Elis). Head of Hera, wearing metal diadem inscribed with letters of her name between palmettes. About 385-365. Silver stater.

2. ALEXANDER, tyrant of Pherae (Thessaly). Head of Hecate, holding torch. 369-357. Silver stater.

3. ACHAEAN LEAGUE. Head of Artemis Laphria (?), hair done on top of her head. About 370. Silver stater.

4. TARENTUM. Head of Demeter, wearing metal diadem and transparent veil ; in front, inscription *Taras* and a dolphin ; behind, signature *E*. (For reverse, see pl. XLII, no. 4.) About 375. Gold stater.

PLATE XXXIV.

1. LOCRI OPUNTII (Central Greece). Head of nymph crowned with water-plant (inspired by the Arethusa of Euaenetus, pl. XXVIII, no. 1). About 369-338. Silver stater.

2. STYMPHALUS (Arcadia). Head of nymph, laureate. About 362-350. Silver stater.

3. MORGANTINA (Sicily). Head of nymph, crowned with water plant inspired by the Arethusa of Euaenetus, pl. XXVIII, no. 1 . (For reverse, see pl. LII, no. 3.) About 367-345. Silver tetradrachm.

4. SYRACUSE. Head of Athena in helmet bound with olive. About 375-357. Bronze litra.

PLATE XXXV.

1. ADRANUM (Sicily). Head of Sikelia, crowned with myrtle. About 345. Bronze litra.

2. METAPONTUM (Lucania). Head of Demeter crowned with corn. About 330-300. Silver stater.

3. AMPHICTIONIC COUNCIL. Head of Demeter of Anthela veiled and crowned with corn. (For reverse, compare pl. XLIII, no. 4.) About 340. Silver stater. Mr. W. H. Woodward.

4. SUCCESSORS of Alexander the Great. Head of Athena in crested helmet adorned with coiled serpent. (For reverse, see pl. XLIV, no. 3.) About 310-300 Gold stater.

PLATE XXXVI.

1. CYME (Aeolis, Asia Minor). Head of the Amazon Cyme, hair bound with fillet. About 190-150. Silver tetradrachm.

2. CNIDUS (Caria). Head of Aphrodite ; behind, monogram of mint-official, *Te.* About 300. Silver tetradrachm.

3. PHILISTIS, Queen of Syracuse. Her portrait, veiled ; behind, a thyrsus bound with a fillet. 269-216. Silver twenty-litra piece.

4. CLEOPATRA VII, Queen of Egypt. Her portrait, diademed. 51-30. Bronze eighty-drachm piece.

PLATE XXXVII.

1. CAULONIA (Bruttium). Apollo (?), wielding a lustral branch, and holding a small running figure with winged. sandals (a wind-god ?). Before him, a stag. Inscription *Kaul*. Guilloche border. About 550-480. Silver stater.

2. POSEIDONIA (afterwards Paestum, Lucania). Poseidon, wielding trident. Inscription *Pos*. About 550-470. Silver stater.

3. CYZICUS (Mysia). Heracles, kneeling, holding bow and wielding club ; behind, a tunny-fish. About 550-470. Electrum stater.

4. OLYMPIA (Elis). Victory, running, carrying wreath and holding up her skirt. Inscription *Wa*. About 510-471. Silver stater.

5. CATANA (Sicily). Victory walking, carrying a wreath of olive. Inscription *Katanaion*. (Reverse of pl. LIX, no. 3.) About 485 to 476. Silver tetradrachm.

6. PEPARETHUS (island near Thessaly). Winged male figure (Agon, the god of athletic contests ?), with winged sandals, running, carrying two wreaths. About 500-478. Silver tetradrachm.

PLATE XXXVIII.

1. NAXOS (Sicily). Silenus squatting on the ground carrying wine-cup to his lips. Inscription *Naxion*. (Reverse of pl. I, no. 2.) About 460. Silver tetradrachm.

2. CATANA (Sicily under the name of Aetna. Zeus of Aetna, on a seat covered with panther's skin, holding thunderbolt and resting his left hand on a vine-staff ; in front, eagle perched on a pine-tree. (Reverse of pl. I. no. 1.) 476-461. Silver tetradrachm. Royal Library, Brussels.

3. POSEIDONIA (afterwards Paestum, Lucania). Poseidon wielding trident. Inscription *Poseidoniatan*. About 480-470. Silver stater.

4. CYZICUS (Mysia). Nude archer, helmeted, kneeling, holding bow and testing an arrow. Behind, a tunny-fish. About 470. Electrum stater. Capt. E. G. Spencer-Churchill.

5. TARENTUM. The founder seated, resting on staff and holding a distaff. Inscription *Taras*. About 473-460. Silver stater.

6. HIMERA (Sicily). The nymph Himera, in transparent chiton, about to put on her mantle. Inscription *Himera*. About 472-460.

PLATE XXXIX.

1. HIMERA (Sicily). The nymph Himera, in chiton and mantle, pouring a libation on an altar ; beside her, a small satyr enjoying a stream of warm water from a lion's-mouth fountain ; in the field, a grain of corn. About 472-450. Silver tetradrachm. Mr. A. H. Lloyd.

2. RHEGIUM (Bruttium). The founder (?) seated, resting on staff ; below his chair, a dog ; inscription *Rheginos*. The whole in a wreath of olive. (Reverse of pl. LIII, no. 3.) About 466-450. Silver tetradrachm.

3. SELINUS (Sicily). The river-god Hypsas, with small horn on forehead, holding lustral branch and pouring libation on an altar of health round which is twined a snake ; behind him, a marsh-bird stalks away ; above, a leaf of selinon (wild celery). Inscription *Hypsas*. About 466-455. Silver didrachm. Capt. E. G. Spencer-Churchill.

4. METAPONTUM. Apollo, nude, holding laurel-sapling and bow. About 470-450. Silver stater.

PLATE XL.

1. SELINUS (Sicily). The river-god Selinos, nude, with small horn on forehead, holding lustral branch and pouring libation on a garlanded altar, before which stands a cock ; behind him, on a pedestal, the statue of a bull (the river Selinos in a more primitive personification) ; above which, a leaf of the selinon-plant (wild celery). Inscription : *Selinos*. (Reverse of pl. XLIX, no. 3.) About 466-455. Silver tetradrachm. Mr. A. H. Lloyd.

2. NAXOS (Sicily). Silenus squatting on the ground, carrying wine-cup to his lips and holding thyrsus ; beside him a vine growing. Inscription : *Naxion*. (Reverse of pl. II, no. 1.) About 450-440. Silver tetradrachm.

3. THEBES. Heracles, beardless, nude, kneeling and stringing his bow. Inscription *Thebaion*. About 441-426.

4. THASOS. Heracles, clad in lion-skin, kneeling to aim with bow and arrow ; before him, a wine-cup. Inscription : *Thasion*. (Reverse of pl. IV, no. 2.) About 411-390. Silver tetradrachm. Capt. E. G. Spencer-Churchill.

PLATE XLI.

1. OLYMPIA (Elis). Victory, her wings outspread, seated on a basis of two steps ; she holds a long palm-branch over her shoulder ; below, a spray of olive. Inscription *Wa*. About 432-421. Silver stater.

2. TERINA (Bruttium). The nymph Terina as Victory, winged, seated on a wine-amphora ; she carries a caduceus in one hand ; on the other is perched a little bird. Inscription *Terinaion*. (Reverse of pl. XXIX, no. 4.) About 425-400. Silver stater.

3. PHENEUS (Arcadia). Hermes seated on a basis of two steps, his broad-brimmed hat slung round his neck ; he holds his caduceus. About 421-362. Scratched on the surface is the word for " vow ", showing that the coin was offered to some god. Silver obol.

4. THASOS. Silenus kneeling, holding wine-cup. About 411-350. Silver quarter-drachm.

5. SELINUS (Sicily). Type similar to that of Pl. XL, no. 1, but of more advanced style ; the altar (which is flaming) is not garlanded, but the base of the bull-statue is. About 415-409. Silver tetradrachm. **Mr. W. H. Woodward.**

6. SEGESTA. The River Crimissus as a youthful hunter, his conical hat slung round his neck, standing with one foot resting on a rock near a terminal statue ; he holds two javelins and is accompanied by two hounds. About 415-409. Silver tetradrachm.

PLATE XLII.

1. CROTON (Bruttium). Heracles, as founder (inscription *Oikistas*), nude, seated on his lion-skin, holding filleted branch and club, before an altar ; behind him, his bow and quiver ; below, two fishes. (For reverse, compare pl. LXIV, no. 1.) About 420-390. Silver stater.

2. APHRODISIAS (Cilicia). Aphrodite, wearing kalathos headdress, seated on a seat flanked by two sphinxes, smelling a flower. About 379 to 374. Silver stater.

3. MAUSSOLLUS, satrap of Caria. The Carian Zeus, holding spear and double-axe. Inscription *Maussollo*. Behind, *K*. 367-353. Struck at Halicarnassus. Silver tetradrachm.

4. TARENTUM (Calabria). Poseidon seated, holding trident ; before him the infant Taras appealing to him with out-stretched arms ; behind him a star and *T*. Inscription *Tarantinon*. On the lower edge, *S* or N. About 375. (Reverse of pl. XXXIII, no. 4.) Gold stater.

5. ARCADIAN LEAGUE. Young Pan, with small horns, seated on a rock, holding his throwing-stick. On the rock, his pipes and inscription *Olym*. (Olympic Games ?) In the field, monogram of *Ark*. About 370-362. Silver stater. **Mr. W. H. Woodward.**

6. STYMPHALUS (Arcadia). Heracles, nude, carrying lion-skin and bow, wielding club against the Stymphalian Birds (which are not shown). Between his legs, *So*. Inscription *Stymphalion*. About 362. Silver stater. **Capt. E. G. Spencer-Churchill.**

PLATE XLIII.

1. PHAESTUS (Crete). Heracles, nude, lion-skin on his arm, attacking with his club the Hydra of Lerna ; a crab about to attack his foot. About 320. Silver stater.

2. PHAESTUS. The young god Welchanos seated in the branches of a tree, holding a cock. Inscription *Welchanos*. About 320. Silver stater.

3. GORTYNA (Crete). Europa or Britomartis seated in a pensive attitude in a tree. (For reverse, see pl. LV, no. 4.) About 320. Silver stater.

4. AMPHICTIONIC COUNCIL. Apollo seated on the omphalos, which is covered with a network of fillets ; he holds long laurel-branch over his shoulder ; beside him, his lyre ; in the field, a small tripod. Inscription *Amphiktionon*. (For obverse, compare pl. XXXV, no. 3.) About 340. Silver stater.

5. LOCRI OPUNTII (Central Greece). Ajax son of Oileus, helmeted, charging with short sword and shield (adorned on the inside with a snake) ; between his legs, a small round shield. Inscription *Opontion*. About 369-338. Silver stater.

PLATE XLIV.

1. LYSIMACHUS, king of Thrace. Athena, seated, holding figure of Victory and spear, resting on her shield ; on the side of her seat, a star ; in front, a torch. Inscription *Basileos Lysimachou*. (For obverse, compare pl. IX, no. 2.) 305-281. Silver tetradrachm.

2. PTOLEMY I SOTER, king of Egypt. Archaistic figure of Athena Promachos, fighting with spear and shield ; in the field eagle on thunderbolt, *Ap* in monogram and *Eu*. Inscription *Alexandrou*. 305-285. Silver tetradrachm.

3. SUCCESSORS OF ALEXANDER. Victory holding wreath and naval standard ; in the field star and monogram. Inscription *Alexandrou*. (Reverse of pl. XXXV, no. 4.) About 310-300. Gold stater.

4. DEMETRIUS POLIORCETES, King of Macedon. On the prow of a war-ship, Victory carrying naval standard and blowing trumpet (as the Victory of Samothrace in the Louvre, commemorating the victory over Ptolemy in 306). 306-283. Silver tetradrachm.

5. DEMETRIUS POLIORCETES. Poseidon wielding trident. Between his legs, monogram of *Her.* ; in front, symbol in shape of double-axe. Inscription *Basileos Demetriou*. (Reverse of no. 4.) 306-283. Silver tetradrachm.

PLATE XLV.

1. DEMETRIUS POLIORCETES. Poseidon resting on trident, his right foot on a rock.

Two monograms and inscription *Basileos Demetriou*. 306-283. (For obverse, compare pl. IX, no. 5.) Silver tetradrachm.

2. SELEUCUS I NICATOR, King of Syria. Zeus, laureate, enthroned, holding eagle and resting on lotus-headed scepte. In the field two monograms and the Seleucid symbol, an anchor. Inscription *Basileos Seleukou*. (Reverse of pl. X no. 1.) 306-280. Silver tetradrachm.

3. PYRRHUS, King of Epirus. Victory carrying trophy and wreath ; in the field, a bull's skull. Inscription *Pyrrhou Basileos*. Struck in Sicily. 278-276. Gold stater.

4. SUCCESSOR OF ALEXANDER. Zeus enthroned, holding eagle and resting on lotus-headed sceptre ; at his feet, a grazing horse ; in field, monogram. Inscription *Alexandrou*. About 310. Silver tetradrachm.

5. ANTIOCHUS I, SOTER, King of Syria. Apollo seated on netted omphalos, resting on bow and holding out an arrow to test its straightness. Below, two monograms. Inscription : *Basileos Antiochou*. 280-261. Silver tetradrachm.

PLATE XLVI.

1. DIODOTUS, King of Bactria. Zeus, with aegis on his arm, hurling a thunderbolt ; before him his eagle and a wreath. Inscription *Basileos Diodotou*. (Reverse of pl. XII, no. 4.) About 250. Gold stater.

2. AETOLIAN League. Figure of the mythical founder Aetolus, his broad hat slung round his neck, sword at side, resting one foot on a rock and leaning on a spear with knotted shaft. Perhaps the statue of Aetolus at Thermon. In the field two monograms. Inscription *Aitolon*. (For obverse compare pl. XIII, no. 1.) About 235-233. Silver stater.

3. MAGNESIA on the Maeander (Ionia). Apollo standing before his tripod on a piece of Maeander pattern, holding a short filleted branch. Inscriptions *Magneton* and *Euphemos Pausaniou* (the magistrate of the year of issue). All in a wreath of laurel. About 190-133. Silver tetradrachm.

4. SELEUCUS II, Callinicus, king of Syria. Apollo, leaning on tripod and sighting an arrow. In front, monogram. Inscription *Basileos Seleukou*. 246-226. Silver tetradrachm.

5. ANTIGONUS GONATAS, king of Macedon. Apollo seated on the prow of a war-ship inscribed *Basileos Antigonou*. Below, monogram and trident-head. About 253 or later. Silver tetradrachm.

PLATE XLVII.

1. SELINUS (Sicily). Heracles attacking the Cretan bull with his club. Inscription *Selino(n)tion*. About 466-455. Silver didrachm. Mr. A. H. Lloyd.

2. MENDE (Macedon). Dionysus, wearing woolly cloak, reclining on the back of a mule, holding a drinking-cup ; below, a grain of corn. About 425. Silver tetradrachm. Capt. E. G. Spencer-Churchill.

3. SYRACUSE. Heracles wrestling with lion. (Reverse of pl. XXIX, no. 2.) About 413-400. Gold hundred-litra piece. Capt. E. G. Spencer-Churchill.

4. MENDE (Macedon). Similar to no. 2, but of more advanced style ; Dionysus faces to front. Below, caduceus and *Ni*. About 425-400. (For reverse see pl. LXII, no. 5.) Silver tetradrachm.

5. HERACLEA (Lucania). Heracles wrestling with lion ; behind him, his club ; between his legs, owl. Inscriptions *Herakleion* and *Kal*. About 380-330. Silver didrachm.

PLATE XLVIII.

1. TARENTUM (Calabria). Taras riding on a dolphin over conventional waves ; he holds a helmet in one hand and rests the other on the dolphin ; inscription *Taras* and, below the dolphin, magistrate's signature, *I*. About 380-345. Silver didrachm.

2. TARENTUM. Similar type, in the opposite sense, between two stars ; he holds the helmet in both hands ; inscription *Taras* and magistrate's signature *Ari*. About 380-345 B. C. Silver didrachm.

3. LAMPSACUS (Mysia). Victory slaying a ram for sacrifice. About 390-350. Gold stater.

4. PHILIP II, king of Macedon. Jockey on horseback, holding a long palm-branch ; below, a thunderbolt (mint-mark) and, still lower, letter *N*. Inscription *Philippou*. 359-336 B. C. Silver tetradrachm.

5. TARENTUM. Horseman striking downwards with spear ; he carries two more and a shield. *Kal*. and three other letters in the field. About 344-334. Silver didrachm. Capt. E. G. Spencer-Churchill.

PLATE XLIX.

1. SYRACUSE. Four-horse chariot (the two off horses indicated by doubling the contours of the two near ones) ; above, Victory hovering to place a wreath on the second horse's head. About 485-478. Silver tetradrachm.

2. ORRHESCII (Pangaean district of Macedon). A man, wearing broad-brimmed hat, carrying two spears and conducting two oxen. Inscription *Orrheskion*. About 500-480. Silver octadrachm.

3. SELINUS (Sicily). Four-horse chariot (two horses doubled as on no. 1) driven by Artemis ; with her, Apollo shooting an arrow. Inscription *Selinontion*. (Obverse of pl. XL, no. 1.) About 466-455. Silver tetradrachm. Mr. A. H. Lloyd.

4. SYRACUSE (the Demareteion). Four-horse chariot ; the heads of three horses shown ; the legs of the two near horses shown separately, those of the third horse doubled ; above, Victory flying to crown the third horse ; below, a lion (for the forces of Africa) running. (Obverse of pl. XX, no. 1.) 480. Commemorating the defeat of the Carthaginians at Himera. Silver decadrachm.

PLATE L

1. SYRACUSE (by Euaenetus). Four-horse chariot driven by bearded charioteer ; above, Victory flying, carrying wreath to crown the charioteer and tablet inscribed *Euaineto*. Below, two dolphins. About 425-413. Silver tetradrachm.

2. GELA Four-horse chariot (outlines of two horses doubled) driven by winged Victory ; above, a wreath of olive ; below, inscription *Geloion*. (Obverse of pl. III, no. 4.) About 413-405. Silver tetradrachm . Royal Library, Brussels.

3. CATANA (Sicily) by Euaenetus. Four-horse chariot turning the goal ; above, Victory flying, carrying wreath to crown the charioteer, and tablet inscribed *Euain*. Below, a crab. (Obverse of pl. IV, no. 4.) About 413-404. Silver tetradrachm. Private collection.

4. SYRACUSE, by Kimon. Four-horse chariot ; Victory alights on the heads of the two near horses to crown the charioteer, who reins them in and looks to front ; below the horses' feet, a fallen goal-post ; lower, an ear of barley. Inscription *Syrakosion*. (Reverse of pl. XXVII, no. 1.) About 413-405 B. C. Silver tetradrachm.

PLATE LI.

1. SYRACUSE, by Kimon. Four-horse chariot, Victory flying to crown the charioteer ; the group is placed on a pedestal, on the upper edge of the cornice of which are traces of the signature *Kimon* ; ranged on and against a step are a helmet, pair of greaves, cuirass and shield, below which the word *Athla* (prizes). The arms taken from the Athenians in the defeat of the Sicilian expedition were given as prizes in the games held to celebrate the Syracusan victory. (For obverse, cp. pl. XXVI, no. 1.) About 413-405. Silver decadrachm. Capt. E. G. Spencer-Churchill.

2. AGRIGENTUM (Sicily). Four-horse chariot turning ; above, an eagle flying carrying a snake in his talons; below, a crab. Inscription *Akragas*. (For reverse, see pl. LVIII, no. 1.) About 413-406. Silver decadrachm. Mr. C. S. Gulbenkian.

PLATE LII.

1. SYRACUSE. Victorious four-horse chariot on pedestal with armour, as on pl. LI, no. 1, modified in various details ; the word *Athla* placed above the shield. (Reverse of pl. XXVIII, no. 2.) About 400-390. Silver decadrachm.

2. AGRIGENTUM (Sicily). Four-horse chariot driven by Victory, turning ; above, vine-branch with grapes ; below, inscription *Akragantinon*. About 413-406. Silver tetradrachm.

3. MORGANTINA (Sicily). Four-horse chariot driven by female charioteer ; Victory flies to crown her (type based on the Syracusan decadrachms, such as pl. LI, no. 1). Below, inscription *Morgantinon*. (Reverse of pl. XXXIV, no. 3.) About 367-345. Silver tetradrachm.

PLATE LIII.

1. ACANTHUS (Macedon). Lion bringing down a bull. Below, a flower. About 500-480. Silver tetradrachm.

2. LEONTINI (Sicily). Lion's head surrounded by four barley-corns. Inscription *Leontinon*. (Reverse of pl. I, no. 3.) About 450. Silver tetradrachm.

3. RHEGIUM (Bruttium). Lion's scalp. (For reverse, see pl. XXXIX, no. 2.) About 466-450. Silver tetradrachm.

4. CNIDUS (Caria). Lion's head and left foreleg. Below, magistrate's name *Eobolo*. (For obverse, see pl. XXXI, no. 3.) About 400-390. Silver tetradrachm.

5. CARTHAGINIANS in Sicily. Lion and palm-tree. Below, Punic inscription " people of the camp ". (For obverse, see pl. XXXI, no. 1.) About 400-370. Silver tetradrachm.

PLATE LIV.

1. VELIA. Lion prowling ; above, inscription *Hyeleton*; below, owl flying. About 390. Silver didrachm. Mr. Stanley Robinson.

2. ERETRIA (Euboea). Cow about to lick its hind leg ; on its back, a bird. (For reverse, see pl. LIX, no. 1.) About 511-490. Silver tetradrachm.

3. LARISA (Thessaly). Mare and foal. Inscription *Larisaion*. About 400-344. Silver drachm.

4. Ionia (perhaps Samos). Forepart of bull, head reverted. About 500. Electrum stater.

5. Cyzicus (Mysia). Bull ; below, tunny-fish. About 500. Electrum stater.

6. Poseidonia (afterwards Paestum, Lucania). Bull. Inscription *Poseida*. (Reverse of pl. XXXVIII, no. 3.) About 480-470. Silver stater.

PLATE LV.

1. Thurium (Lucania). Bull about to charge. Below, a fish. Inscription *Thourion*. About 400-450. Silver distater.

2. Samos (island off Ionia). Forepart of bull, with ornamented fillet round shoulders ; behind, an olive-branch. Inscription *Sa*. About 439-408. Silver tetradrachm.

3. Thurium (by Phrygillus). Bull about to charge ; between his feet, artist's signature *Phry*. ; below, a fish ; inscription *Thourion*. About 425. Silver stater.

4. Gortyna (Crete). Bull foreshortened, licking its flank. Inscription *Gortynion*. (Reverse of pl. XLIII, no. 3.) About 320. Silver stater.

PLATE LVI.

1. Messana (Sicily). Hare springing ; below, head of young Pan, and his pipes. Inscription *Messanion*. About 461-396. Silver tetradrachm.

2 Aenus (Thrace). He-goat ; in front, drinking-horn in the form of the forepart of a stag. Inscription. *Ainion*. (Reverse of pl. V, no. 2.) About 421-365. Silver tetradrachm. Capt. E. G. Spencer-Churchill.

3. Ephesus (Ionia). Forepart of stag, the head reverted, and palm-tree. Name of magistrate *Aristodemos*. (For obverse see pl. LIX, no. 3.) About 387-300. Silver tetradrachm.

4. Caulonia (Bruttium). Stag ; in the field, ivy-spray with berries. Inscription *Kauloniatan*. About 400. Silver stater.

5. Augustus. Heifer. Struck in the Eastern provinces. 27-20 B. C. (Reverse of Plate XVIII, no. 4.) Aureus.

PLATE LVII.

1. Agrigentum (Sicily). Eagle. Inscription *Akragantos*. (For reverse, see Plate LIX, no. 2.) About 472-450. Silver tetradrachm.

2. Athens. Owl ; behind, olive-spray and crescent. Inscription *Athe*. (Reverse of Plate XX, no. 2.) About 470. Silver tetradrachm.

3, OLYMPIA (Elis). Eagle tearing a hare. About 432-421. Silver stater.

4. OLYMPIA. Head of eagle; below, an ivy leaf. About 421-365. Silver stater. Mr. W. H. Woodward.

PLATE LVIII.

1. AGRIGENTUM (Sicily). Two eagles on a dead hare, one lifting up its head to shriek, the other bending down. In the field, a locust. (Reverse of pl. LI, no. 2.) About 413-406. The design illustrates a famous passage in the *Agamemnon* of Aeschylus, describing the omen of two eagles feeding on a hare (vv. 110-120). Silver decadrachm. Mr. C. S. Gulbenkian.

2. AGRIGENTUM. Similar to no. 1, but without the locust. Inscription *Akrag.* (For reverse, see Plate LXI, no. 1.) About 413-406. Silver tetradrachm. Formerly in the Ashburnham Collection.

3. CLAZOMENAE (Ionia). Swan beating its wings. Inscription *Klazo.* and magistrate's name *Mandronax.* (Reverse of pl. V, no. 4.) About 387-300. Silver tetradrachm.

PLATE LIX.

1. ERETRIA (Euboea). Cuttle-fish; to left, letter E. (Reverse of pl. LIV, no. 2.) About 511-490. Silver tetradrachm.

2. AGRIGENTUM (Sicily). Crab; below, rose (?) with two curling shoots. (Reverse of pl. LVII, no. 1.) About 472-450. Silver tetradrachm.

3. EPHESUS (Ionia). Bee; inscription *Eph.* (Obverse of pl. LVI, no. 3.) About 387-300. Silver tetradrachm.

4. ATHENS. Mask of the Gorgon Medusa About 561-546. Silver didrachm.

5. NEAPOLIS (Macedon). Mask of the Gorgon Medusa. About 500-411. Silver stater.

PLATE LX.

1. CHIOS (island off Ionia). Sphinx seated; in front, a wine-jar, over which a bunch of grapes. About 431-412. Silver tetradrachm.

2. GELA (Sicily). Forepart of the river-god Gelas, represented as a bull with human face. Inscription Gelas. About 500-466. Silver tetradrachm.

3. CATANA (Sicily). The river-god Amenanus, as a bull with human face; above, a water-fowl (to represent the surface) and below, a fish (to represent the depths of the stream). (Obverse of Plate XXXVII, no. 5.) About 485-476. Silver tetradrachm.

4. AUGUSTUS. Sphinx seated. (Reverse of Plate XVIII, no. 3.) Struck in Asia Minor (Pergamum ?) 27-20 B. C. Silver cistophorus.

PLATE LXI.

1. AGRIGENTUM (Sicily). The marine monster Scylla, her waist girt with dogs, on the look-out for prey ; above, a crab. Inscription *Akragantinon*. (For obverse, see pl. LVIII, no. 2.) About 413-406. Silver tetradrachm, formerly in the Ashburnham Collection.

2. ABDERA (Thrace). Gryphon seated ; in front small nude Silenus. Magistrate's name *Smor*. About 512-478. Silver tetradrachm.

3. TEOS (Ionia). Gryphon seated ; in front, mask of bearded satyr. About 494-394. Silver stater.

4. PANTICAPAEUM (Crimea). Gryphon, with lion's head, horned, holding a spear in his jaws ; below, an ear of corn. Inscription *Pan*. (Reverse of pl. VIII, no. 4.) About 350. Gold stater.

PLATE LXII.

1. CORINTH. Pegasus, bridled, flying ; below, letter *Q*. About 400-350. Silver stater.

2. SICYON (Achaea). Chimaera, with lion's head and body, forepart of goat rising from its back, and tail ending in snake's head. Below, small head of horned river-god (Asopus ?). About 400-323. Silver stater.

3. RHODES. Rose, rose-bud on right, vine-branch, grapes and letter *E* on left ; inscription *Rhodion*. (Reverse of pl. V, no. 3.) About 400-333. Gold stater.

4. RHODES. Rose, with rose-bud on right, small sphinx seated on left. Inscription *Rhodion*. (Reverse of pl. V, no. 5.) About 400-333. Silver tetradrachm.

5. MENDE (Macedon). Vine, conventionalized, in a linear square, surrounded by inscription *Mendaion*. (Reverse of pl. XLVII, no. 4.) About 425-400. Silver tetradrachm.

PLATE LXIII.

1. METAPONTUM (Lucania). Ear of barley. Inscription *Meta*. About 550-500. Silver stater.

2. BARCE (Cyrenaica). Three stems of silphium-plant conjoined, accompanied by owl, chamaeleon and jerboa. Inscription *Barkaion*. Silver tetradrachm.

3. METAPONTUM. Ear of barley, with leaf, on which sits a field-mouse ; below, letter *Ph*. Inscription *Meta*. About 350-330. Silver stater.

4. ALEXANDER son of Neoptolemus, king of Epirus. Thunderbolt ; beside it, a spear-head. Inscription *Alexandrou tou Neoptolemou.* (Reverse of pl. IX, no. 3.) 342-326. Gold stater.

5. OLYMPIA (Elis). Thunderbolt on the inside of a shield ; inscription *Wa.* About 421-365. Silver stater.

PLATE LXIV.

1. CROTON (Bruttium) Delphic tripod, with rings round the bowl, and fillets hanging from it ; across it Apollo shoots an arrow at the Python. (For obverse, compare pl. XLII, no. 1.) About 420-390. Silver stater.

2. TISSAPHERNES, Persian satrap in Caria (?). Lyre. Inscription *Basil.* " coin of the King ". (Reverse of pl. VII, no. 3.) About 395. Silver tetradrachm.

3. THEBES. Crater (wine-mixer) with volute handles ; above, open rose. Across field *Epami.* (Epaminondas, the Theban leader.) About 378-335. Silver stater.

4. AMPHIPOLIS (Macedon). Race-torch ; in the field, letter *A* ; inscription on a broad rectangular frame, *Amphipoliton.* (Reverse of pl. VI, no. 1.) About 424-358. Silver tetradrachm.

LIST OF PLATES

Plate

I. — 1. CATANA (Sicily). — 2. NAXOS (Sicily). — 3. LEONTINI (Sicily). — 4. CATANA (Sicily).

II. — 1. NAXOS (Sicily) — 2. CAMARINA (Sicily). — 3. MYTILENE (Lesbos). — 4. AENUS (Thrace). — 5. CATANA (Sicily).

III. — 1. CHALCIDICE (Macedon). — 2. CHALCIDICE (Macedon). — 3. MARONEA (Thrace). — 4. GELA (Sicily).

IV. — 1. OLYMPIA (Elis). — 2. THASOS (island off Thrace). — 3. RHEGIUM (Bruttium). — 4. CATANA (Sicily).

V. — 1. CATANA (Sicily). — 2. AENUS (Thrace). — 3. RHODES. — 4. CLAZOMENAE (Ionia). — 5. RHODES.

VI. — 1. AMPHIPOLIS (Macedon). — 2. CYRENE (N. Africa). — 3. SYBRITA (Crete). — 4. SYBRITA (Crete).

VII. — 1. LAMPSACUS (Mysia). — 2. LAMPSACUS (Mysia). — 3. TISSAPHERNES. — 4. CYZICUS (Mysia). — 5. CYZICUS (Mysia).

VIII. — 1. CYRENE (N. Africa). — 2. ARCADIAN FEDERATION. — 3. PHILIP II. — 4. PANTICAPAEUM (Crimea). — 5. OLYMPIA (Elis). — 6. PHILIP II.

IX. — 1. ALEXANDER THE GREAT. — 2. LYSIMACHUS. — 3. ALEXANDER SON OF NEOPTOLEMUS. — 4. PTOLEMY I SOTER. — 5. DEMETRIUS POLIORCETES.

X. — 1. SELEUCUS I NICATOR. — 2. PHILETAERUS. — 3. ANTIOCHUS I SOTER. — 4. PTOLEMY I SOTER.

XI. — 1. EUMENES I. — 2. HIERO II.

XII. — 1. BAGADAT. I — 2. SELEUCUS II CALLINICUS. — 3. ANTIOCHUS HIERAX. — 4. DIODOTUS.

XIII. — 1. AETOLIAN LEAGUE. — 2. MITHRADATES III. — PHILIP V.

XIV. — 1. PHARNACES I. — 2. PERSEUS.

XV. — 1. EUTHYDEMUS II. — 2. OROPHERNES.

XVI. — 1. DEMETRIUS I SOTER. — 2. ANTIMACHUS.

XVII. — 1. ANTIOCHUS VI. DIONYSUS. — 2. HELIOCLES.

XVIII. — 1. MITHRADATES VI EUPATOR THE GREAT. — 2. TIGRANES THE GREAT. — 3. AUGUSTUS. — 4. AUGUSTUS.

XIX. — 1. ATHENS. — 2. SYRACUSE. — 3. SYRACUSE. — 4. CORINTH.

XX. — 1. SYRACUSE (the Demareteion). — 2. ATHENS. — 3. SYRACUSE. — 4. CNIDUS (Caria).

XXI. — 1. SYRACUSE. — 2. SYRACUSE. — 3. SYRACUSE. — 4. SYRACUSE.

XXII. — 1. SYRACUSE. — 2. SYRACUSE. — 3. SYRACUSE. — 4. SYRACUSE.

XXIII. — 1. SYRACUSE. — 2. SYRACUSE. — 3. SYRACUSE. — 4. THURIUM (Lucania).

Plate

XXIV. — 1. SYRACUSE (by Euaenetus). — 2. SYRACUSE (by Eumenos). — 3. SYRACUSE (by Eucleidas). — 4. SYRACUSE (by Phrygillus).

XXV. — 1. SYRACUSE. — 2. SYRACUSE (by Eucleidas). — 3. SYRACUSE. — 4. SYRACUSE.

XXVI. — 1. SYRACUSE (by Kimon). — 2. SYRACUSE (by Kimon).

XXVII. — 1. SYRACUSE (by Kimon). — 2. SYRACUSE. — 3. SYRACUSE. — 4. NEAPOLIS (Macedon).

XXVIII. — 1. SYRACUSE (by Euaenetus). — 2. SYRACUSE (by an unknown artist).

XXIX. — 1. SYRACUSE (by Euaenetus). — 2. SYRACUSE. — 3. SEGESTA (Sicily). — 4. TERINA (Bruttium). — 5. EUBOEA.

XXX. — 1. METAPONTUM (Lucania). — 2. METAPONTUM. — 3. METAPONTUM. — 4. METAPONTUM.

XXXI. — 1. CARTHAGINIANS IN SICILY. — 2. CARTHAGINIANS IN SICILY. — 3. CNIDUS. — 4. LARISA (Thessaly).

XXXII. — 1. THURIUM (Lucania). — 2. VELIA (Lucania). — 3. CORINTH. — 4. LAMPSACUS (Mysia). — LAMPSACUS (Mysia).

XXXIII. — 1. OLYMPIA (Elis). — 2. ALEXANDER, tyrant of Pherae (Thessaly). — 3. ACHAEAN LEAGUE. — 4. TARENTUM.

XXXIV. — 1. LOCRI OPUNTII (Central Greece). — 2. STYMPHALUS (Arcadia). — 3. MORGANTINA (Sicily). — 4. SYRACUSE.

XXXV. — 1. ADRANUM (Sicily). — 2. METAPONTUM (Lucania). — 3. AMPHIOTICNIC COUNCIL. — 4. SUCCESSORS of Alexander the Great.

XXXVI. — 1. CYME (Aeolis, Asia Minor). — 2. CNIDUS (Caria). — 3. PHILISTIS. — 4. CLEOPATRA VII.

XXXVII. — 1. CAULONIA (Bruttium). — 2. POSEIDONIA (afterwards Paestum, Lucania). — 3. CYZICUS (Mysia). — 4. OLYMPIA (Elis). — 5. CATANA (Sicily). — 6. PEPARETHUS (island near Thessaly).

XXXVIII. — 1. NAXOS (Sicily). — 2. CATANA (Sicily). — 3. POSEIDONIA (afterwards Paestum, Lucania). — 4. CYZICUS (Mysia). — 5. TARENTUM. — 6. HIMERA (Sicily).

XXXIX. — 1. HIMERA (Sicily). — 2. RHEGIUM (Bruttium). — 3. SELINUS (Sicily). — 4. METAPONTUM.

XL. — 1. SELINUS (Sicily). — 2. NAXOS (Sicily). — 3. THEBES. — 4. THASOS.

XLI. — 1. OLYMPIA (Elis). — 2. TERINA (Bruttium). — 3. PHENEUS (Arcadia). — 4. THASOS. — 5. SELINUS (Sicily). — 6. SEGESTA (Sicily).

XLII. — 1. CROTON (Bruttium). — 2. APHRODISIAS (Cilicia). — 3. MAUSSOLLUS. — 4. TARENTUM (Calabria). — 5. ARCADIAN LEAGUE. — 6. STYMPHALUS (Arcadia).

XLIII. — 1. PHAESTUS (Crete). — 2. PHAESTUS. — 3. GORTYNA (Crete). — 4. AMPHICTIONIC COUNCIL. — 5. LOCRI OPUNTII (Central Greece).

XLIV. — 1. LYSIMACHUS. — 2. PTOLEMY I SOTER. — 3. SUCCESSORS OF ALEXANDER. — 4. DEMETRIUS POLIORCETES. — 5. DEMETRIUS POLIORCETES.

XLV. — 1. DEMETRIUS POLIORCETES. — 2. SELEUCUS I NICATOR. — 3. PYRRHUS. — 4. SUCCESSOR OF ALEXANDER. — 5. ANTIOCHUS I SOTER.

XLVI. — 1. DIODOTUS. — 2. AETOLIAN LEAGUE. — 3. MAGNESIA on the Maeander (Ionia). — 4. SELEUCUS II Callinicus. — 5. ANTIGONUS GONATAS.

Plate

XLVII. — 1. SELINUS (Sicily). — 2. MENDE (Macedon). — 3. SYRACUSE. — 4. MENDE (MACE-
DON). — 5. HERACLEA (Lucania).

XLVIII. — 1. TARENTUM (Calabria). — 2. TARENTUM. — 3. LAMPSACUS (Mysia). — 4. PHILIP
II. — 5. TARENTUM.

XLIX. — 1. SYRACUSE. — 2. ORRHESCII (Pangaean district of Macedon). — 3. SELINUS
(Sicily). — 4. SYRACUSE (the Demareteion).

L. — 1. SYRACUSE (by Euaenetus). — 2. GELA. — 3. CATANA (Sicily). — 4. SYRACUSE
(by Kimon).

LI. — 1. SYRACUSE (by Kimon). — 2. AGRIGENTUM (Sicily).

LII. — 1. SYRACUSE. — 2. AGRIGENTUM (Sicily). — 3. MORGANTINA (Sicily).

LIII. — 1. ACANTHUS (Macedon). — 2. LEONTINI (Sicily). — 3. RHEGIUM (Bruttium). —
4. CNIDUS (Caria). — 5. CARTHAGINIANS in Sicily.

LIV. — 1. VELIA. — 2. ERETRIA (Euboa). — 3. LARISA (Thessaly). — 4. IONIA (perhaps
Samos). — 5. CYZICUS (Hysia). — 6. POSEIDONIA (afterwards Paestum,
Lucania).

LV. — 1. THURIUM (Lucania). — 2. SAMOS (island off Ionia). — 3. THURIUM (by Phrygillus). — 4. GORTYNA (Crete).

LVI. — 1. MESSANA (Sicily). — 2. AENUS (Thrace). — 3. EPHESUS (Ionia). — 4. CAULONIA
(Bruttium). — 5. AUGUSTUS.

LVII. — 1. AGRIGENTUM (Sicily). — 2. ATHENS. — 3. OLYMPIA (Elis). — 4. OLYMPIA.

LVIII. — 1. AGRIGENTUM (Sicily). — 2. AGRIGENTUM. — 3. CLAZOMENAE (Ionia).

LIX. — 1. ERETRIA (Euboea). — 2. AGRIGENTUM (Sicily). — 3. EPHESUS (Ionia). —
4. ATHENS. — 5. NEAPOLIS (Macedon).

LX. — 1. CHIOS (island off Ionia). — 2. GELA (Sicily). — 3. CATANA (Sicily). — 4. AUGUS-
TUS.

LXI. — 1. AGRIGENTUM (Sicily). — 2. ABDERA (Thrace). — 3. TEOS (Ionia). — 4. PAN-
TICAPAEUM (Crimea).

LXII. — 1. CORINTH. — 2. SICYON (Achaea). — 3. RHODES. — 4. RHODES. — 5. MENDE
(Macedon).

LXIII. — 1. METAPONTUM (Lucania). — 2. BARCE (Cyrenaica). — 3. METAPONTUM. —
4. ALEXANDER son of Neoptolemus. — 5. OLYMPIA (Elis).

LXIV. — 1. CROTON (Bruttium). — 2. TISSAPHERNES. — 3. THEBES. — 4. AMPHIPOLIS
(Macedon).

CONTENTS

Page

Preface.. 5

Introduction 7

Description of the plates... 35

List of plates... 59

———

THE PRINTING OF THIS BOOK WAS COMPLETED
ON DECEMBER SECOND OF THE YEAR NINETEEN
HUNDRED AND TWENTY SIX, BY THE IMPRIMERIE
PROTAT FRÈRES, MACON, FOR G. VANOEST,
PUBLISHER AT PARIS AND BRUSSELS. COLLOTYPE
PLATES PRINTED BY LÉON MAROTTE, PARIS.
PHOTOGRAPHS BY DONALD MACBETH, LONDON.

Pl. II

1

2

3

4

1

2

3

4

5

Hélio Léon Marotte Paris

1

2

3

4

Hélio Léon Marotte Paris

Pl. VII

1

2

3

4

5

Hélio Léon Marotte Paris

Pl. VII

PL. VIII

1

2

3

4

5

6

Hélio Léon Marotte Paris

Pl. VIII

1

2

3

4

5

1

2

3

4

Hélio Leon Marotte Paris

1

2

Hélio Léon Marotte Paris

1

2   3

4

Hélio Léon Marotte Paris

1

2

3

Hélio Léon Marotte Paris

1

2

1

2

Hélio Léon Marotte Paris

1

2

Pl. XVII

1

2

Hélio Léon Marotte Paris

Pl. XVII

Pl. XVIII

Hélio Léon Marotte Paris

Pl. XIX

1

2

3

4

Hélio Léon Marotte Paris

1

2

3

4

Hélio Léon Marotte Paris

1

2

3

4

Hélio Léon Marotte Paris

Pl. XXIII

Pl. XXIV

Pl. XXV

1

2

3

4

Hélio Léon Marotte, Paris

1

2

Hélio Léon Marotte Paris

Pl. XXVII

Pl. XXVIII

1

2

Hélio Léon Marotte Paris

Pl. XXIX

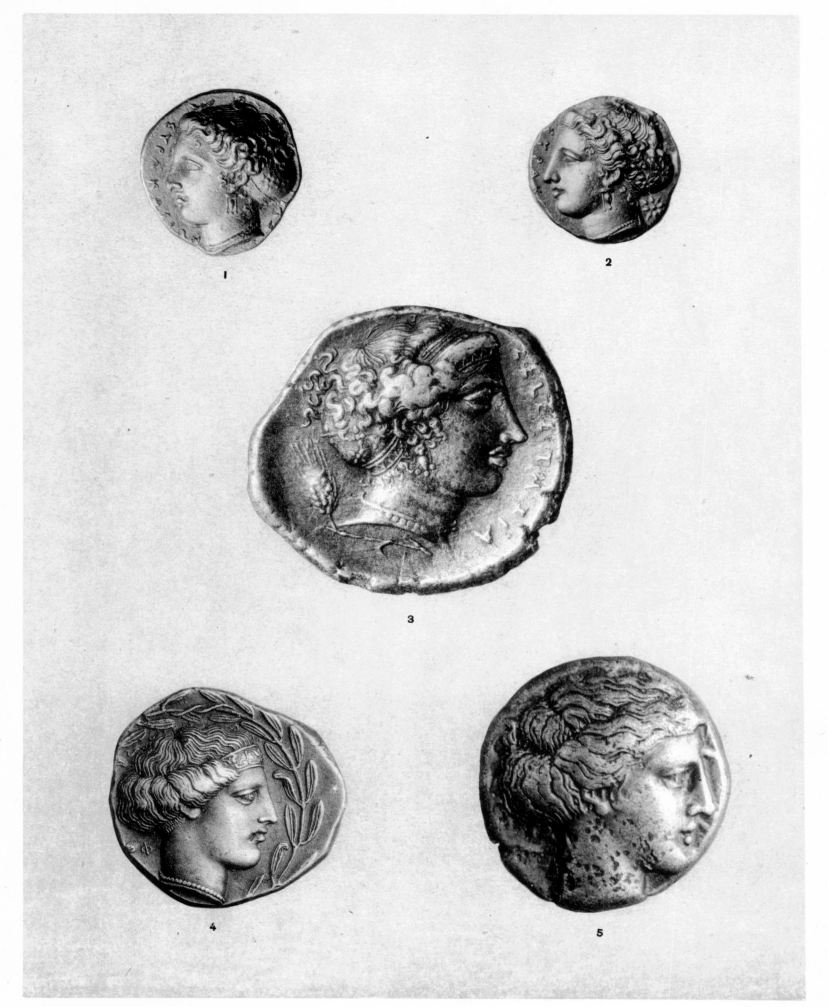

Hélio Léon Marotte Paris

1

2

3

4

Hélio Léon Marotte Paris

Hélio Léon Marotte Paris

Hélio Léon Marotte Paris

1

2

3

4

Hélio Léon Marotte Paris

1

2

3

4

5

6

Hélio Léon Marotte Paris

Pl. XXXVII

Pl. XL

Pl. XLI

1

2

3

4

5

6

1

2

3

4

5

Pl. XLVIII

Pl. XLVIII

1

2

3

4

Hélio Léon Marotte Paris

Pl. L

Hélio Léon Marotte Paris

Pl. I.

Pl. LI

1

2

1

2

3

Hélio Léon Marotte Paris

1

2

3

4

5

Hélio Léon Marotte Paris

1

2

3

4

5

6

Pl. LV

1

2

3

4

Hélio Léon Marotte Paris

1

2

3

4

5

Hélio Léon Marotte Paris

1

2

3

Hélio Léon Marotte Paris

Pl. LIX

Pl. LX

Pl. IX

Pl. LXI

1

2

3

4

Hélio Léon Marotte Paris

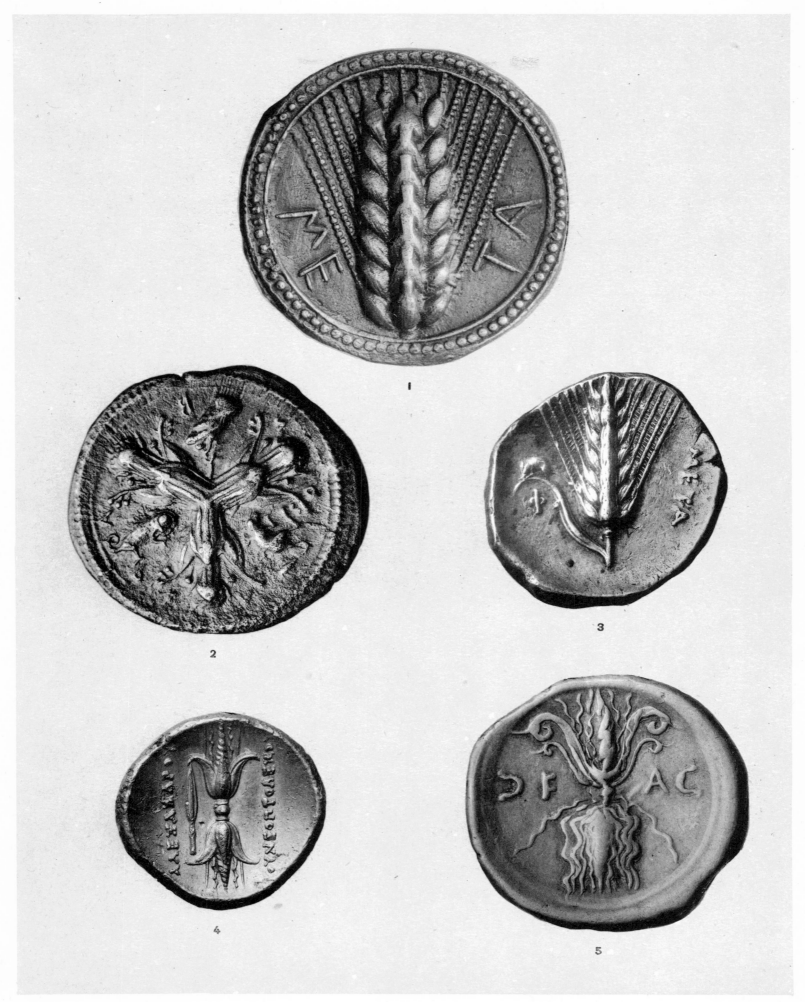

Hélio Léon Marotte Paris